Martin B. Brown

An Act to Reorganize the Local Government of the City of New York,

Passed April 30, 1873 as Amended

Martin B. Brown

An Act to Reorganize the Local Government of the City of New York,
Passed April 30, 1873 as Amended

ISBN/EAN: 9783744734912

Printed in Europe, USA, Canada, Australia, Japan

Cover: Foto ©Suzi / pixelio.de

More available books at **www.hansebooks.com**

TO

REORGANIZE THE LOCAL GOVERNMENT

OF THE

CITY OF NEW YORK,

Passed April 30, 1873,

AS AMENDED;

With an Appendix containing the

SUPPLEMENTARY ACTS

Passed since the Year 1873.

———◆———

NEW YORK:

MARTIN B. BROWN, PRINTER AND STATIONER,

Nos. 201, 203 & 205 William Street,

———

1876.

BOARD OF ALDERMEN.

AUGUST 10, 1876.

———◆———

The following resolution was adopted :

Resolved, That one thousand copies of the act, chapter 335, Laws of 1873, commonly called the Charter, with the acts amendatory thereof, be printed in document form, for the use of the Mayor, members of the Common Council, and other city officials, under the direction of the Clerk.

FRANCIS J. TWOMEY,

Clerk.

CONTENTS OF CHARTER.

ARTICLE I.

PAGE.

The Corporate Powers.................................... 1

ARTICLE II.

Of the Legislative Powers......... 1

ARTICLE III.

Of the Executive Power.... 14

ARTICLE V

Of the Finance Department................................ 22

ARTICLE VI.

Of the Law Department................................... 32

ARTICLE VII.

Of the Police Department................................. 34

ARTICLE VIII.

Of the Department of Public Works........................ 48

ARTICLE IX.

PAGE.

Of the Department of Public Charities and Correction............ 53

ARTICLE X.

Of the Fire Department 55

ARTICLE XI.

Of the Health Department........... 57

ARTICLE XII.

Of the Department of Public Parks........................... 60

ARTICLE XIII.

Of the Department of Buildings...,,....................... 62

ARTICLE XIV.

Of the Department of Taxes and Assessments.................. 63

ARTICLE XV.

Of the Department of Docks................. 64

ARTICLE XVI.

General Provisions, Powers and Limitations. 64

CONTENTS OF APPENDIX.

(A.)—Chapter 515, Laws of 1874.

PAGE.

Amending section 4 of chapter 335 of Laws of 1873, relating to office and election of aldermen 105

(B.)—Chapter 304, Laws of 1874.

Act consolidating the government of the city and county of New York 107

(C.)—Chapter 305, Laws of 1874.

Act explanatory of act to consolidate the government of the city and county of New York 108

(D.)—Chapter 757, Laws of 1873.

Amending various sections of act reorganizing the local government of the city of New York............................. 109

(E.)—Chapter 159, Laws of 1875.

Amending section 35 of chapter 335 of Laws of 1873, relating to the city chamberlain..................................... 116

(F.)—Chapter 300, Laws of 1874.

Amending section 39 of chapter 335, Laws of 1873, relating to the police department....................................... 118

(G.)—Chapter 476, Laws of 1875.

Relating to an uniform system for pavement of streets, avenues, and public places 120

(H.)—CHAPTER 726, LAWS OF 1873.

PAGE.

An act for the more effectual extinguishment of fires............ 121

(I.)—CHAPTER 839, LAWS OF 1873.

An act authorizing new contract for removal of contents of sinks
and privies... 122

(J.)—CHAPTER 759, LAWS OF 1873.

An act providing for new commissioners in matter of completion
of county buildings....... 124

(K)—CHAPTER 631, LAWS OF 1875.

Amending section 19 of chapter 757, Laws of 1873, relating to
printing and supplies of stationery........................... 125

(L.)—CHAPTER 758, LAWS OF 1873.

An act authorizing board of estimate and apportionment to
revise, etc., tax rates for 1873. 126

(M.)—CHAPTER 308, LAWS OF 1874.

An act authorizing a revision of the estimates for 1874.......... 127

(N.)—CHAPTER 303, LAWS OF 1874.

An act further authorizing a revision of the estimates for 1874.
and granting to board power of transferring appropriations ... 130

(O)—CHAPTER 326, LAWS OF 1873.

An act limiting the effect of certain repealing clauses of act of
1873, relating to prior rights, indictments and prosecutions.... 132

Chapter 335.

An Act to reorganize the local government of the city of New York.

Passed April 30, 1873; three-fifths being present.

The People of the State of New York, represented in Senate and Assembly, do enact as follows:

ARTICLE I.

The Corporate Powers.

SECTION 1. The corporation now existing and known by the name of "The Mayor, Aldermen, and Commonalty of the city of New York" shall continue to be a body politic and corporate, in fact and in name, by the same name, and have perpetual succession, with all the grants, powers, and privileges heretofore held by the mayor, aldermen, and commonalty of the city of New York, and not modified or repealed by the provisions of this act. *Corporate powers.*

ARTICLE II.

Of Legislative Powers.

SEC. 2. The legislative power of the said corporation shall continue to be vested in a board of aldermen and a board of assistant aldermen, who together shall form the *Legislative powers.*

1

Assistant aldermen, board of, abolished. common council of the city of New York. The board of assistant aldermen is hereby abolished from and after the first day of January, eighteen hundred and seventy-five; and from and after that date the board of aldermen is hereby declared to be the common council, and shall solely possess the powers and perform all the duties by law conferred or imposed upon the board of aldermen, and board of assistant aldermen, the common council, or any one or more of them.

SEC. 3. Such aldermen shall be elected as hereinafter provided.

Aldermen, election of. SEC. 4. [*As amended by sec.* 1, *chap.* 515, *laws of* 1874.] The board of aldermen now in office shall hold office until the first Monday in January, in the year eighteen hundred and seventy-five, the same being the term for which they were elected. There shall be twenty-two aldermen elected at the general state election which shall occur in the year eighteen hundred and seventy-four, three of whom shall be elected in each senate district, except the eighth senate district, and shall be residents of the district in which they are elected, but no voter shall vote for **Aldermen in twenty-third and twenty-fourth wards.** more than two of said aldermen. In the territory comprised within the eighth senate district, and the twenty-third and twenty-fourth wards, there shall be elected four aldermen, and the aldermen to be elected in said district may reside either in said eighth senate district or in the twenty-third and twenty-fourth wards, but no voter shall vote for more than three of the said aldermen. There shall also **Aldermen at large.** be elected six aldermen at large to be voted for on a separate ballot, but no voter shall vote for more than four of the said aldermen at large, and the voters of the twenty-third and twenty-fourth wards of said city are hereby authorized and empowered to vote for aldermen at large. The members of the board of aldermen shall hold office for the space of one year, and shall take office on the first Monday in January, next succeeding their election, at noon. Annually **Annual election.** thereafter, at the general state election, there shall be elected a full board of aldermen as hereinbefore provided. Any vacancy now existing or which may **Vacancies, how filled.** hereafter occur in *either* the board of aldermen* by reason of the death or resignation, or of any other cause, of a member of either of said boards, shall be filled by election by the board in which such vacancy exists or shall arise, by a vote of a majority of all the members elected to said board; and the person so elected to fill any such vacancy shall serve until the first day of January, at noon, next succeeding the first general election occurring not less than thirty days after the happening of such vacancy, but not beyond the expiration of the term in which the vacancy shall occur; and at such election a person shall be elected to serve the remainder, if any, of such unexpired term. From and after the termination of the term of

* So in the original.

office of the board of assistant aldermen, as herein provided, the board of aldermen alone shall constitute the common council and shall exercise the entire legislative powers of the said city.*

Quorum.

SEC. 5. The boards shall meet in separate chambers, and a majority of each shall constitute a quorum; but the comptroller, the commissioner of public works, the corporation counsel, and the president of each department shall be entitled to seats in each board, and to notice of its meetings, and shall have the right to participate in the discussions of each board, but in nowise shall be considered as members of either board, and shall not have the right to vote in either board.

SEC. 6. Each board shall—

Officers, how elected.

1. Choose a president from its own members by a call of the names of the members of the board, upon which call each member shall announce his choice, and when once chosen he can be removed before the expiration of his term as alderman or assistant alderman only, by a vote, taken by a call of ayes or noes, of four-fifths of all the members of the board of which he shall have been chosen president;

Powers and duties.

2. Appoint a clerk and other officers;

3. Determine the rules of its own proceedings;

4. Be the judge of the election returns and qualifications

*See Appendix, A, B. and C.

of its own members, subject, however, to the review of any court of competent jurisdiction;

5. Keep a journal of its proceedings;

6. Sit with open doors;

7. Have the authority to compel the attendance of absent members, and to punish its members for disorderly behavior, and to expel any member, with the concurrence of two-thirds of the members elected to the board.

But no alderman or assistant alderman shall sit or act as a magistrate in any judicial matter or proceeding. This section, however, shall not be construed to require or authorize a reorganization of the existing board of aldermen, or board of assistant aldermen. *Aldermen denied judicial powers.*

SEC. 7. [*As amended by sec. 2, chap. 757, laws of 1873.*] Every member expelled from either board shall thereby forfeit all his rights and powers as alderman or assistant alderman.*

SEC. 8. [*As amended by sec. 3, chap. 757, laws of 1873.*] The stated and occasional meetings of each board shall be regulated by its own resolutions and rules, and both boards may meet at the same time or on different days, as they may severally deem expedient. *Meetings.*

SEC. 9. Every legislative act of the common council shall be by resolution or ordinance; and every ordinance *All acts to be approved by Mayor.*

*See Appendix, D.

or resolution shall, before it shall take effect, be presented, duly certified, to the mayor for his approval.

SEC. 10. [*As amended by sec.* 4, *chap.* 757, *laws of* 1873.] The mayor shall return such ordinance or resolution to the board in which it originated within ten days after receiving it, or at the next meeting of such board after the expiration of said ten days.

Veto. SEC. 11. If he approve it, he shall sign it. If he disapprove it, he shall specify his objections thereto in writing. If he do not return it with such disapproval within the time above specified, it shall take effect as if he had approved it.

Veto to be entered in journal. SEC. 12. Such objections of the mayor shall be entered at large on the journal of the board in which said ordinance or resolution originated.

Proceedings in case of a veto. SEC. 13. The board to which such ordinance or resolution shall have been returned, with objections, shall, after ten days and within fifteen days after such ordinance or resolution shall have been so returned, proceed to reconsider and vote upon the same; and if the same shall, on reconsideration, be again passed by both boards by the votes of at least two-thirds of all the members elected to each board, but in no case by a less vote than was neces_ sary on its first passage, it shall take effect. But if the ordinance or resolution shall fail to receive, upon the first vote thereon, such number of affirmative votes, it shall be Votes, how taken. deemed finally lost. In all cases the vote shall be taken by ayes and noes, and the names of the persons voting for or against its passage, on such reconsideration, shall be entered in the journal of each board. In case an ordinance or resolution shall embrace more than one distinct subject, the mayor may approve the provisions relating to one or more subjects and disapprove the others. In such case, those which he shall approve shall become effective, and those which he shall not approve shall be reconsidered by the board, and shall only become effective if again passed as above provided.

Sec. 14. Any ordinance or resolution may originate in either board, and when it shall have passed one board, may be rejected or amended in the other; but no ordinance or resolution shall be passed except by a vote of the majority of all the members elected to the board, and no ordinance or resolution shall be valid unless it shall receive the assent of both boards within the term fixed by law to such boards. In case any ordinance or resolution involves the expenditure of money or the laying of an assessment, the lease of real estate or franchises, the votes of three-fourths of all the members elected to each board shall become necessary to its passage. No money shall be expended for any celebration, procession, funeral ceremony, reception or entertainment of any kind, or on any occasion, unless by the votes of four-fifths of all the members elected to each board. No additional allowance beyond the legal claim which shall exist under any contract with the corporation, or with any department or officer thereof, or for any

Ordinances may originate in either board.

Expenditure limited.

services on its account or in its employment, shall ever be passed by the common council, except by the unanimous vote thereof; but, in all cases, the provisions of any such contract shall determine the amount of any claim thereunder or in connection therewith, against the said corporation, or the value of any such services.

Clerk of board, his powers and duties.

SEC. 15. [*As amended by sec. 5, chap. 757, laws of 1873.*] The clerk of the board of aldermen shall, by virtue of his office, be clerk of the common council and of the board of supervisors, and shall perform all the duties heretofore performed by the clerk of the common council, except such as shall be assigned to the clerk of the board of assistant aldermen, without additional compensation to that paid him as clerk of the board of aldermen. It shall be his duty to keep open for inspection, at all reasonable times, the records and minutes of the proceedings of said boards. He shall keep the seal of the city, and his signature shall be necessary to all leases, grants and other documents, as under existing laws. The clerk of each board shall, subject to the rules of the board, appoint and remove at pleasure deputy clerks in his department and fix their salaries. The deputy clerks and other officers of the board of aldermen shall be officers of the board of supervisors, which shall have no separate officers or subordinates, and such clerks and officers shall receive no additional compensation for duties performed for the supervisors. The aggre-

Deputy clerks.

gate amount of salaries paid to the clerks and officers Salaries.
of the board of aldermen, including the salary of the
clerk, shall not exceed twenty-five thousand dollars
in any one year, and the aggregate amount of salaries
paid to the clerks and officers of the board of assistant aldermen, including the salary of the clerk, shall
not exceed fifteen thousand dollars in any one year.

SEC. 16. Immediately after the adjournment of each To prepare and publish abstract of meetings.
meeting of either board, it shall be the duty of the clerk of
such board to prepare a brief abstract, omitting all technical
and formal details, of all resolutions and ordinances intro-
duced or passed, and of all recommendations of committees,
and of all final proceedings, as well as full copies of all
messages from the mayor, and all reports of departments
or officers. He shall at once transmit the same to the
person appointed to supervise the publication of the City
Record. No resolution or ordinance providing for or Resolutions to be published.
contemplating the alienation or appropriation or leasing
any property of the city, terminating the lease of any
property or franchise, or the making of any specific improvement, or the appropriation or expenditure of public
moneys, or authorizing the incurring of any expense or
the taxing or assessing of property in the city, shall be
passed or adopted by either board until at least five days
after such abstract of its provisions shall have been
published. No such ordinance or resolution shall be
approved by the mayor until three days after such abstract
shall have been so published after its passage; but if an

abstract of any resolution or ordinance shall have been once published after its introduction, it shall not thereafter be necessary to publish the same again, but only to refer to the date and page of the former in the City Record, and to state the amendments, if any, made thereto. In all cases the yeas and nays upon the final passage of the resolution or ordinance shall be published. The

City Record to be certified and deposited. comptroller shall cause a continuous series of the City Record to be bound as completed quarterly, and to be deposited, with his certificate thereon, in the office of the register of deeds in the city and county of New York, in

County clerk's office. the county clerk's office and in the office of the clerk of the common council, and copies of the contents of any part of the same, certified by such register, county clerk, or clerk of the common council, shall be received in judicial proceedings as prima facie evidence of the truth of the contents thereof.

Powers of common council. SEC. 17. The common council shall have power to make, continue. modify, and repeal such ordinances, regulations and resolutions as may be necessary to carry into effect any and all of the powers now vested in or by this act conferred upon the corporation, and shall have the power to enforce obedience to such ordinances and observance thereof, by ordaining penalties for each and every violation thereof, in such sums as it may deem expedient, not exceeding one hundred dollars ; and shall have power to make such ordinances, not inconsistent with law and the constitution of this state, and with such penalties, in the matter, and for the purposes following, in addition to other powers elsewhere specially granted, namely:

1. To regulate traffic and sales in the streets, highways, roads and public places. *Powers specified.*

2. To regulate the use of the streets, highways, roads and public places by foot passengers, animals, vehicles, cars and locomotives. *Use of streets.*

2.* To regulate the use of sidewalks, and prevent the extension of building fronts and house fronts within the stoop lines. *Use of sidewalks.*

4. To prevent encroachments upon and obstructions to the streets, highways, roads and public places, not including parks, and to authorize and require the commissioners of public works to remove the same, but they shall have no power to authorize the placing or continuing of any encroachment or obstruction upon any street or sidewalk, except the temporary occupation thereof, during the erection or repair of a building on a lot opposite the same. *Obstructions.*

5. To regulate the opening of street surfaces, the laying of gas and water mains, the building and repairing of sewers, and the erecting of gas-lights. *Opening streets.*

6. To regulate the numbering of the houses and lots in the streets and avenues, and the naming of the streets, *To number houses.*

*So in original.

avenues and public places; but it shall not be lawful for the said board to number or renumber any houses, in any street, avenue, alley, lane, road, way or public place, or to in anywise change or alter any such numbering or the name of any street, avenue or public place, save between the first day of December of any year and the first day of May next ensuing.

Garbage, etc.

7. To regulate and prevent the throwing or depositing of ashes, offal, dirt or garbage in the streets.

Cleaning streets.

8. To regulate the cleaning of the streets, avenues, sidewalks and gutters, and removing ice and snow from them.

Use of streets.

9. To regulate the use of the streets and sidewalks for signs, sign-posts, awnings, awning-posts, horse-troughs, urinals, telegraph-posts and other purposes.

10. [*As amended by sec. 6, chap. 757, Laws of 1873.*] To provide for and regulate street pavements, crosswalks, curbstones, gutterstones, sidewalks, and the grade of streets, and to provide for regulating, grading, flagging, curbing, guttering and lighting streets, roads, places and avenues.

To regulate street traffic, etc.

11. To regulate public cries, advertising noises, steam whistles, and ringing bells in the streets, and to control and limit traffic in the streets, avenues and public places.

12. In relation to street beggars, vagrants and mendicants.

13. In relation to the use of guns, pistols, firearms, firecrackers, fireworks, and detonating works of all descriptions within the city.

14. In relation to intoxication, fighting and quarreling in the streets.

15. In relation to places of public amusement.

16. In relation to exhibiting banners, placards or flags in or across the streets or from houses or other buildings.

17. In relation to the exhibition of advertisements or handbills along the streets, avenues and public places.

18. In relation to the construction, repairs and use of vaults, cisterns, areas, hydrants pumps and sewers.

19. In relation to partition fences and walls.

20. In relation to the construction, repair, care and use of markets.

21. In relation to the licensing and business of public *Licensing hackmen.* cartmen, truckmen, hackmen, cabmen, expressmen, cardrivers, boatmen, pawnbrokers, junk dealers, hawkers, peddlers and venders, and all licenses shall be according to an established form and regularly numbered, and be duly registered in the office of the mayor.

22. In relation to the inspection and sealing of weights and measures, and enforcing the keeping and use of proper weights and measures by venders.

23. In relation to the inspection, weighing and measur-

ing of fire-wood, coal, hay and straw, and the cartage of the same.

24. In relation to the mode and manner of suing for, collecting and keeping accounts of the city and county, and disposing of the penalties provided for a violation of all ordinances.

Public fountains. 25. In relation to the erection and repair of public fountains for the use of man and animals, at convenient points along the streets and avenues and public places.

26. By resolution to require the commissioner of public works to do any work or take any action proper for carrying into effect the powers of the common council. The ordinances of the common council shall, as far as practicable, be reduced to a code, and be published as such in the City Record.

To impose taxes. SEC. 18. The common council shall have no power to impose taxes or assessments, or borrow money, or contract debts, or loan the credit of the city, or take or make a lease of any real estate or franchise, save at a reasonable rent and for a period not exceeding five years, unless specially authorized so to do by act of the legislature.

ARTICLE III.
Of the Executive Power.

SEC. 19. The executive power of the corporation shall be vested in the mayor and the officers of the departments herein created.

SEC. 20. [*As amended by sec. 7, chap.* 757, *laws of*
1873.] The mayor in office on April twenty-ninth,
eighteen hundred and seventy-three, shall hold office
until the first day of January, in the year eighteen
hundred and seventy-five. The mayor shall be the
chief executive officer of the corporation; shall be
elected at a general election, and hold his office for
the term of two years, commencing on the first day
of January next after his election. The first election
for mayor under this act shall be at the general
election in November, in the year eighteen hundred
and seventy-four.

SEC. 21. Whenever the mayor shall be under suspension, or there shall be a vacancy in the office of mayor,
or whenever, by reason of sickness or absence from the
city, he shall be prevented from attending to the duties
of his office, the president of the board of aldermen shall
act as mayor, and possess all the rights and powers of
mayor during such suspension, disability or absence. In
case of a vacancy he shall so act until the first Monday of
January succeeding the next general election, and at the
general election next to be held, at which a mayor can be
chosen, but not within ten days after the occurrence of
any such vacancy, a mayor shall be chosen for the unexpired term for which such officer was chosen, and no
special election shall be held to fill such vacancy. It
shall not be lawful for the president of the board of
aldermen when acting as mayor, in consequence of the

sickness or absence from the city of the person elected, to exercise any power of appointment to or removal from office, unless such sickness or absence of the mayor shall have continued ten days, nor to sign, approve, or disapprove any ordinance or resolution, unless such sickness or absence shall have continued the same period.

Temporary chairman in case of vacancy.

SEC. 22. In case of a vacancy in the office of mayor, the aldermen may elect a temporary chairman to preside over their meetings, who shall possess, during such vacancy, the powers and perform the duties of the president of the board.

SEC. 23. It shall be the duty of the mayor:

Mayor to make annual statement.

1. To communicate to the common council, at least once a year, a general statement of the finances, government and improvements of the city.

2. To recommend to the common council all such measures as he shall deem expedient.

3. To keep himself informed of the doings of the several departments.

4. To be vigilant and active in causing the ordinances of the city and laws of the state to be executed and enforced, and for that purpose he may call together for consultation and co-operation all heads of departments.

5. And generally to perform all such duties as may be prescribed for him by the city ordinances and the laws of the state.

Sec. 24. The mayor may appoint such clerks and subor- dinates as he may require to aid him in the discharge of his official duties, and shall render to the board of aldermen, every three months, an account of the expenses and receipts of his office, and therein shall state, in detail, the amounts paid and agreed to be paid by him for salaries to such clerks and subordinates respectively, and the general nature of their duties, which shall be published in the City Record. The aggregate expenses incurred by him for such purposes shall not exceed, in any one year, the sum of twenty thousand dollars.

Sec. 25. The mayor shall nominate, and, by and with the consent of the board of aldermen, appoint the heads of departments and all commissioners (save commissioners of public instruction, and also save and except the following named commissioners and officers who held office as such on the first day of January, in the year one thousand eight hundred and seventy-three, that is to say, the comptroller, the commissioner of public works, the counsel to the corporation, the president of the department of public parks, and the president of the department of police, which said comptroller, commissioners and counsel to the corporation shall hold their respective offices, as such comptroller, commissioners and counsel to the corporation aforesaid, until the expiration of their respective terms of office for which they were appointed, unless removed for cause as herein provided), and the said mayor shall in like manner appoint all members of any board or com-

2

mission authorized to superintend the erection or repair of any building belonging to or to be paid for by the city, whether named in any law or appointed by any local authority, and also members of any other local board and all other officers not elected by the people,* including the commissioner of jurors, whose appointment is not in this act excepted or otherwise provided for. Every head of department and person in this section named, except as herein otherwise provided, shall hold his office for the term of six years, and in each case until a person is duly appointed in his place. The terms of office of all such heads of departments and persons other than those first appointed shall commence on the first day of May, but the heads of departments, consisting of boards of commissioners first appointed after the passage of this act, shall, except as herein otherwise expressly provided, be appointed, for two, four and six years respectively, and except that the commissioners of police first appointed as aforesaid shall hold their offices for one, two, three and five years respectively. The persons first appointed shall take office on the expiration of the terms of office of the present incumbents, as hereinafter provided, and shall hold their offices until the first day of May in the year in which it is herein provided that their respective terms shall expire. All nominations to any office or offices which, by this act, the mayor is authorized or empowered to nominate a person or persons to in place of any present incumbent or incumbents, shall be made to the board of

Terms of office.

Nominations.

* See Appendix, D.

aldermen within twenty days after the passage of this act, and any such nomination or nominations to fill any vacancy which shall hereafter occur by reason of the expiration of the term of office of any officer, or from any other cause, and which shall not be created by anything in this act, providing for the termination of the term of office of any officer or person now in office, shall be made to the board of aldermen, within ten days from the day of the date of any such vacancy, and any person who shall be appointed to fill any such vacancy shall hold his office for the unexpired term of his predecessor. The mayor may be removed from office by the governor in the same manner as sheriffs, except that the governor may direct the inquiry provided by law to be conducted by the attorney-general; and after charges have been received by the governor he may, pending the investigation, suspend the mayor for a period not exceeding thirty days. The heads of all departments, including those retained as above, and all other persons whose appointment is in this section provided for, may be removed by the mayor for cause, and after opportunity to be heard, subject, however, before such removal shall take effect, to the approval of the governor, expressed in writing. The mayor shall, in all cases, communicate to the governor, in .writing, his reasons for such removal. Whenever a removal is so effected, the mayor shall, upon the demand of the officer removed, make, in writing, a public statement of the reasons therefor. No officer so removed shall

Mayor, how removed.

Heads of departments, how removed.

be again appointed to the same office during the same term of office.

[As amended by sec. 3, chap. 300, laws of 1874.]

Mayor to fill vacancy.

The mayor of said city shall hereafter appoint, without confirmation of the board of aldermen, a person or persons to fill any vacancy or vacancies which now exists or may hereafter occur from death, resignation or cause other than the expiration of the full term in any office to which, of the provisions of the twenty-fifth section of chapter three hundred and thirty-five of the laws of eighteen hundred and seventy-three, he is empowered to appoint by and with the consent of the board of aldermen.*

City departments.

Sec. 26. There shall be the following other departments in said city :

Finance department.

Law department.

Police department.

Department of public works.

Department of public charities and correction.

Fire department.

Health department.

Department of public works. †

Department of docks.

* See Appendix, F.　　† So in original.

Department of taxes and assessments.

Department of buildings.

SEC. 27. The said departments shall, once in three months, and at such other times as the mayor may direct, make to him, in such form and under such rules as he may prescribe, reports of the operations and action of the same and each of them, which reports shall be published in the City Record. The said departments shall always, when required by the mayor, furnish to him such information as he may demand, within such reasonable time as he may direct.

SEC. 28. The heads of all departments (except as otherwise herein specifically provided) shall have power to appoint and remove all chiefs of bureaus (except the chamberlain), as also all clerks, officers, employees, and subordinates in their respective departments, except as herein otherwise specially provided, without reference to the tenure of office of any existing appointee. But no regular clerk or head of a bureau shall be removed until he has been informed of the cause of the proposed removal, and has been allowed an opportunity of making an explanation; and in every case of a removal, the true grounds thereof shall be forthwith entered upon the records of the department or board. In case of removal, a statement, showing the reason therefor, shall be filed in the department. The number and duties of all officers and clerks, employees and subordinates in every department, except as otherwise herein specifically provided, with their respective salaries, whether now fixed by special law or otherwise, shall be such as the heads of the respective departments shall designate and approve; but subject, also, to the revision of the board of apportionment; provided, however, that the aggregate expense thereof shall not exceed the total amount duly appropriated to the respective departments for such purposes. Any head of department may, with the consent of the board of apportionment, consolidate any two or more bureaus established by law, and may change the duties of any bureau; and it shall be the duty of the head of the finance department to bring together all officers and bureaus authorized to receive money for taxes, assessments or arrears, in such manner that the payment of the same can be made, as nearly as practicable, at one time and place, and in one office.

ARTICLE V.

Of the Finance Department.

Finance. Sec. 29. The finance department shall have control of the fiscal concerns of the corporation. It shall prescribe the forms of keeping and rendering all city accounts, and, except as herein otherwise provided, the manner in which all salaries shall be drawn, and the mode by which all creditors, officers and employees of the corporation shall be paid. All payments by or on behalf of the corporation shall be made through the proper disbursing officer of the department of finance, on vouchers to be filed in said department, by means of warrants drawn on the chamberlain by the comptroller, and countersigned by the mayor. The comptroller may require any person presenting for settlement an account or claim against the corporation to be sworn before him touching such account or claim, and when so sworn to answer orally as to any facts relative to the justness of such account or claim. The power hereby given the comptroller to settle and adjust such claims shall not be construed to give such settlement and adjustment the binding effect of a judgment or decree, nor to authorize the comptroller to dispute the amount of any salary established by or under the authority of any officer or department authorized to establish the same nor to question the due performance of his duties by such officer, except when necessary to prevent fraud. The comptroller shall not reduce the rate of interest upon any taxes or assessments below the amount fixed by law. No contract hereafter made, the expense of the execution of which is not by law or ordinance in whole or in part to be paid by assessments upon the property benefited, shall be binding or of any force or effect unless the comptroller shall indorse thereon his certificate that there remains unexpended and unapplied, as herein provided, a balance of the appropriation applicable thereto sufficient to pay the estimated expense of executing such contract as certified by the officer making the same.

Claimants to be sworn.

Contracts, how binding.

[*Amended by sec.* 8, *chap.* 757, *laws of* 1873.]

But this provision shall not apply to work done, or supplies furnished, not involving the expenditure of more than one thousand dollars, pursuant to section ninety-one of this act. It shall be the duty of the comptroller to make such indorsement upon every such contract so presented to him, if there remains unapplied and unexpended such amount so specified by the officer making the contract, and to thereafter hold and retain such sum to pay the expense incurred until the said contract shall be fully performed. And such indorsement shall be sufficient. evidence of such appropriation in any action. The comptroller shall furnish to each head of department, weekly, a statement of the unexpended balance of the appropriation for his department; wages and salaries, including payments for the board of education, may be made upon pay-rolls, upon which each person named thereon shall separately receipt for the amount paid to such person, and in every case of payment upon a pay-roll, the warrant for the aggregate amount of wages and salaries included therein, may be made payable to the superintendent, principal teacher, foreman or other officer designated for the purpose.

SEC. 30. The head of the finance department shall be called the comptroller of the city of New York, and shall hold his office for four years, and until his successor shall be appointed, unless sooner removed as herein provided.

Comptroller
to furnish
weekly
statement.

Pay-rolls.

Comptroller,
term of
office.

SEC. 31. All accounts rendered to or kept in the other Accounts subject to departments shall be subject to the inspection and revision revision. of the officers of this department; and, subject to the conditions aforesaid, it shall settle and adjust all claims in favor of or against the corporation, and all accounts in which the corporation is concerned as debtor or creditor, but, in adjusting and settling such claims, it shall, as far as practicable, be governed by the rules of law and principles of equity which prevail in courts of justice.

SEC. 32. The comptroller of the city of New York Deputy comptroller. shall appoint, and at pleasure remove, for cause to be stated in writing and published in said City Record, a deputy comptroller. The said deputy comptroller shall, in addition to his other powers, possess every power and perform all and every duty belonging to the office of comptroller, as herein provided, whenever the said comptroller shall, for reasons to be stated to the mayor in writing, by due written authority, and during a period of time not extending beyond three months, nor beyond his term of office, and to be specified in such authority, designate and authorize the said deputy comptroller to possess the power and perform the duty aforesaid, and such designation and authority shall be duly filed in and remain of record in the finance department and in the mayor's office. The said deputy comptroller shall possess Powers and duties. the like authority in case of the disability of the comptroller upon the like designation of the mayor, which shall be filed and remain of record as aforesaid;

but such authority may at any time be terminated in the same manner as it was created.

Bureaus. SEC. 33. There shall be eight bureaus in this department:

Collection of revenues.

1. A bureau for the collection of the revenue accruing from rents, and interest on bonds and mortgages, revenue arising from the use or sale of property belonging to or managed by the city; the chief officer of which bureau shall be called the "collector of the city revenue."

2. A bureau for the collection of taxes; the chief officer of which shall be called the "receiver of taxes," and he shall have all the powers, and perform all the duties heretofore prescribed by law for the receiver of taxes.

3. A bureau for the collection of arrears of taxes and assessments and of water rents; the chief officer of which shall be called "clerk of arrears."

4. An auditing bureau, which, under the supervision of the comptroller, shall audit, revise, and settle all accounts in which the city is concerned as debtor or creditor, and which shall keep an account of each claim for or against the corporation, and of the sums allowed upon each, and certify the same to the comptroller, with the reasons for the allowance; the chief officer of which shall be called "auditor of accounts."

5. A bureau of licenses; the chief officer of which shall be called "register of licenses."

6. A bureau of markets; the chief officer of which shall be called "superintendent of markets."

7. A bureau for the reception of all moneys paid into the treasury of the city, and for the payment of money on warrants drawn by the comptroller and countersigned by the mayor; the chief officer of which shall be called the "chamberlain."

8. A bureau for the collection of assessments; the chief officer of which shall be called "collector of assessments," and his assistants "deputy collectors of assessments."

SEC. 34. The chamberlain shall be appointed in the same manner as heads of departments, and shall hold his office for four years, unless sooner removed, as herein provided. He shall, within ten days after receiving notice of his appointment and confirmation, and before he enters upon his office, give a bond to the city in the sum of one million dollars, with not less than four sufficient sureties, to be approved by the comptroller, conditioned that he will faithfully execute the duties of his office. Such bond shall be deemed to extend to the faithful execution of the duties of the office until a new appointment shall be made and confirmed, and the person so appointed enters upon the performance of his duties. Said chamberlain shall exhibit to the common council at its first meeting in the

(margin notes: Appointment of chamberlain. To give bond. Duties of.)

month succeeding that in which he enters upon the
execution of his office, an exact statement of the balance
in the treasury to the credit of the city, with a summary
of the receipts and payments of the treasury during the
preceding year, and since the last preceding report
required by law, if more than a year shall have elapsed
since such report. He shall receive all moneys which
shall, from time to time, be paid into the treasury of the
city. He shall deposit all moneys which shall come into
his hands on account of the city on the day of the receipt
thereof, or on the business day next succeeding, in such
banks and trust companies as shall have been designated
as deposit banks by the chamberlain and mayor jointly;
but not exceeding two millions dollars shall be on deposit
at any time in any one bank or trust company. The
money so deposited shall be placed to the account of the
chamberlain, and he shall keep a bank book, in which
shall be entered his accounts of deposits in, and moneys
drawn from, the banks and trust companies in which the
deposits shall be made. The said banks and trust

Weekly
statement of
deposits.

companies shall, respectively, transmit to the comptroller
a weekly statement of the moneys which shall be received
and paid by them on account of the city treasury. The
chamberlain shall pay all warrants drawn on the treasury
by the comptroller and countersigned by the mayor, and
no moneys shall be paid out of the treasury except on the
warrant of the comptroller so countersigned. No such
warrant shall be signed by the comptroller or countersigned by the mayor, except upon vouchers for the

expenditure of the amount named therein, examined and
allowed by the auditor, approved by the comptroller, and
filed in the department of finance, except in the case of
judgments, in which case a transcript thereof shall be filed,
nor except such warrant shall be authorized by law or
ordinance, and shall refer to the law or ordinance and to
the appropriation under and from which it is drawn. The
chamberlain shall not draw any moneys from said banks
or trust companies, unless by checks subscribed by him as
chamberlain and countersigned by the comptroller; and
no moneys shall be paid by either of the said banks or
trust companies on account of the treasury except upon
such checks. The chamberlain shall exhibit his bank Monthly
statement.
book to the comptroller on the first Tuesday of every
month, and oftener when required. The accounts of the
city treasury shall be annually closed on the last day of
November, and shall be examined in the month of
December in said year by the commissioners of accounts.
Such commissioners shall examine the accounts and Annual
account.
vouchers of all moneys received into and paid out of the
city treasury during the year ending on the last day of
November next preceding such examination, and shall
certify and report to the mayor and the common council,
in the following month of January, the amount of moneys
received into the treasury during such year, the amount of
moneys paid out during the same period by virtue of
warrants drawn on the treasury by the comptroller, the
amount of moneys received by the chamberlain who shall
be in office at the time of such examination if he entered

upon the execution of his duties since the last preceding report, the balance in the treasury on the last day of November preceding such examination, the amount of moneys borrowed for or on the credit of the city during such year, and the amount of bonds of the city issued during such year, with the purposes for which and the authority under which such bonds were issued. Such commissioners shall also compare the warrants drawn by the comptroller on the treasury during the year ending on the last day of November preceding such examination, with the several laws and ordinances under which the same shall purport to have been drawn, and shall in like manner certify and report whether the comptroller had power to draw such warrants ; and if any shall be found which in their opinion he had no power to draw, they shall specify the same in their report, with their reasons for such opinion.

Warrants to be compared.

SEC. 35. [*As amended by sec.* 1, *chap.* 129, *laws of* 1875.] The said chamberlain and mayor and the comptroller of the city of New York shall, by a majority vote, by written notice to the comptroller, designate the banks or trust companies in which all moneys of the mayor, aldermen, and commonalty of the said city and county of New York shall be deposited, and may, by like notice, in writing, from time to time, change the banks or trust companies thus designated; but no such bank or trust company shall be designated unless its officers shall agree to pay

Banks, how chosen.

into the city treasury interest on the daily balances at
a rate to be fixed by the mayor and chamberlain and
the said comptroller of the city of New York by a
majority vote, which rate shall not be less than two
and one-half per cent. The said chamberlain shall
keep books showing the receipts of moneys from all
sources, and designating the sources of the same, and
also showing the amounts paid from time to time on
acccount of the several appropriations; and no warrant shall be paid on account of any appropriation
after the amount authorized to be raised for that
specific purpose shall have been expended. The said *Weekly report.*
chamberlain shall once in each week report in writing
to the mayor and to the comptroller all moneys received by him, the amounts of all warrants paid by
him since his last report, and the amount remaining
to the credit of the city and county of New York
respectively. The said chamberlain shall receive the *Salary.*
sum of thirty thousand dollars annually and no more
for all his services as chamberlain of said city and as
county treasurer of the county of New York in lieu
of salary and of all interest, fees, commissions and
emoluments; and all such interest, fees, commissions
and emoluments shall be accounted for and paid over
by him to the city treasury. He may appoint and *Clerks.*
remove at pleasure a deputy chamberlain and such
clerks and assistants as may be necessary, whose
salaries, together with all the expenses of his office,
shall be paid wholly by him, and shall in no case be

a public charge. The commissions provided by law
and received by him for receiving and paying over
the state taxes and all interest accrued on deposits
shall be paid by him to the commissioners of the
sinking fund.*

ARTICLE VI.

Of the Law Department.

SEC. 36. The law department shall have the charge and
conduct of all the law business of the corporation and its
departments, and of all law business in which the city of
New York shall be interested, except as herein otherwise
provided; the charge and conduct of the legal proceedings necessary in widening, opening or altering streets,
and the preparation of all leases, deeds and other legal
paper connected with any department. No officer or
department, except as herein otherwise provided, shall
have or employ any attorney or counsel, but it shall be
the duty of the law department to furnish to every department and officer such advice and legal assistance as counsel or attorney, in or out of court, as may be required by

such officer or department; and for that purpose he may
assign an attorney to any department that he shall deem
to need the same, and may appoint the attorney for the
collection of personal taxes.

SEC. 37. The head of the law department shall be

* See Appendix, E.

called "counsel to the corporation." He shall hold his office for four years, and until his successor is appointed, unless sooner removed, as herein provided.

SEC. 38. There shall be two bureaus in this department, Bureaus. the chief officer of one of which shall be called the "corporation attorney," and the chief officer of the other of which shall be called the "public administrator." Such chief officers shall not receive to their own use any fees or emoluments in addition to their salaries, and they shall pay into the treasury all costs and commissions received by them from any source whatever; such payments shall be made monthly, and shall be accompanied by a sworn statement, in such form as the comptroller shall prescribe, and that such statement, with a detailed list of costs, commissions, fines and penalties collected, shall be published in the City Record monthly, as furnished. All Actions, how actions to recover penalties for a violation of any law or brought. ordinance shall be brought in the name of the mayor, aldermen and the commonalty of the city of New York, and not in that of any department, and shall be conducted by the corporation attorney, subject to the control of the corporation counsel. All fees received in said action Fees shall be paid into the treasury of the city. The counsel to the corporation shall, once in three months, report to Quarterly report. the comptroller the names of parties to, and the objects of, all suits pending in his department, when commenced, and the number decided or ended, and in what manner, during the past three months.

3

ARTICLE VII.

Of the Police Department.*

Police commissioners.

SEC. 39. [*As amended by sec.* 1, *chap.* 300, *laws of* 1874.] The police department shall have for its head a board to consist of four persons, to be known as police commissioners of the city of New York, who shall, except those first appointed, hold their offices for six years, unless sooner removed as herein provided. The office of the police commissioner of the city of New York, whose term of office expires on the first day of May, eighteen hundred and seventy-four, is hereby abolished on and after said date; the police department, on and after the first day of May, eighteen hundred and seventy-four, shall be under the charge and control of four commissioners, who shall perform all the duties and exercise all the powers now by law conferred or imposed upon the police department of the city of New York.

Police force

SEC. 40. The police force shall be appointed by said board, and shall be composed of a superintendent and three inspectors, and as many captains of police, sergeants of police, patrolmen and doormen of police, and as many clerks and employees of police as the Board of police may, from time to time, determine and the funds appropriated allow, except that the number of patrolmen shall not be

* See Appendix, F, and sec. 1, chap. 755, Laws of 1873.

increased in any one year more than one hundred beyond the number authorized the previous year. The Board of Police surgeons. police may appoint not exceeding twenty-two surgeons of police, one of whom shall be designated as chief surgeon. They shall detail from the force, to be under direction of the mayor, not exceeding six patrolmen.

SEC. 41. The government and discipline of the police Government and discipline. department shall be such as the Board may, from time to time, by rules and regulations, prescribe, but members of the police force shall be removable only after written charges shall have been preferred against them, and after the charges have been publicly examined into, upon such reasonable notice to the person charged, and in such manner of examination as the rules and regulations of the board of police may prescribe. The clerks and employees Clerks. shall, except as herein otherwise provided, be appointed and removed at pleasure by the board of police, according to fixed rules to be established by the board.

SEC. 42. The board of police may, by resolution Retired list on pension. adopted by the unanimous vote of a full board, setting forth the reasons therefor under such rule, retire from office, in such police department or force, any inspector, captain, sergeant, patrolman or surgeon (if disabled while in the actual performance of duty), and place the person so retired upon the pension-roll of the police life insur ance fund, and allow him an annual retiring pension not exceeding in amount one-third the annual salary or com pensation of such office. But no such inspector, captain, sergeant, surgeon or patrolman shall be so retired from office and placed on the pension-roll except at his own request in writing, unless due notice is given him of the intention so to retire ; nor unless it shall be certified to the board by two of the police surgeons that he is, in their opinion, permanently, mentally, or physically incapacitated from duty as such inspector, captain, sergeant, surgeon, or patrolman ; nor unless the said board shall concur in such opinion ; nor unless the nature and origin of such incapacity shall be stated in the resolution so retiring him.

Present force and pay continued.

SEC. 43. Every person connected with the police department of the city of New York, at the time this act shall take effect, and except as otherwise herein ordered, shall continue in office, and the amount of salary or compensation now legally paid to such person, except as herein otherwise provided or authorized, shall be the salary and compensation fixed for his office under this act ; but the commissioners to be appointed under this act may fix the salary and compensation of such clerks other than policemen whom they may be authorized by law to employ.

Qualifications for membership.

SEC. 44. No person shall ever be appointed to membership in the police force, or to continue to hold membership therein, who is not a citizen of the United States, or who has ever been convicted of crime, or who cannot read and write understandingly in the English language, or who shall not have resided within the city and state one year, but skilled officers of experience may be appointed for detective duty who have not resided as herein required. The name, residence, and occupation of each applicant for appointment to any position in the police department, as well as the name, residence, and occupation of each person appointed to any position, shall be published, and such publication shall, in every instance, be made on the Saturday next succeeding such application or appointment, in the City Record.

Appointments to be published.

SEC. 45. The board of police may, upon an emergency or apprehension of riot, tumult, mob, insurrection, pestilence, or invasion, appoint as many special patrolmen without pay from among the citizens as it may deem desirable. The board of police, with the approbation in writing of the mayor, or, in case of their disagreement, the governor may, under similar circumstances, demand the assistance of the military of the first division, or of any brigade, regiment, or company thereof, by order in writing, served upon the commanding officer of such division, and such commanding officer shall obey such order.

Special patrolmen.

Military assistance.

SEC. 46. During the service of any special patrolman authorized as aforesaid, he shall possess all the powers and privileges, and perform all the duties that may be by orders, rules, and regulations from time to time prescribed. Every such special patrolman shall wear a badge, to be prescribed and furnished by the board of police.

Powers of special patrolmen.

Resigna-
tions

SEC. 47. No member of the police force, under penalty of forfeiting the salary or pay which may be due him, shall withdraw or resign, except by permission of the board of police. Unexplained absence, without leave, of any member of the police force, for five days, shall be deemed and held to be a resignation of such member, and accepted as such.

Police board
may issue
subpœnas,
examine wit-
nesses, etc.

SEC. 48. The board of police shall have power to issue subpœnas, tested in the name of its president, to compel the attendance of witnesses upon any proceedings authorized by its rules and regulations. Each commissioner of police, the superintendent thereof, and the chief clerk and deputy thereof, are hereby authorized and empowered to administer affirmations and oaths to any person summoned and appearing in any matter or proceeding, authorized as aforesaid, and in all matters pertaining to the department or the duties of any officer, or to take any depositions necessary to be made under the orders, rules, and regulations of the board of police, or for the purposes of this act. Any person making a complaint that a felony or misdemeanor has been committed may be required to make affirmation or oath thereto, and for this purpose the inspectors. captains, and sergeants of police shall have power to administer affirmations and oaths.

False swear-
ing.

Any willful or corrupt false swearing, by any witness or person, to any material fact in any necessary proceeding under the said orders, rules, and regulations, or under this act, shall be deemed perjury, and punished in the manner now prescribed by law for such offense. The provisions and procedure of chapter thirty-nine of the laws of eighteen hundred and sixty, passed February eighteen, eighteen hundred and sixty, are hereby applied to the case of any witness subpœnaed under this section.

SEC. 49. The board of police may, with the authority and approval of the mayor and the common council, from time to time, but with special reference to locating the same as centrally in precincts as possible, establish, provide, and furnish stations and station-houses, or sub-stations and sub-station-houses, at least one to each precinct, for the accommodation thereat of members of the police force, and as places of temporary detention for persons arrested and property taken within the precinct; and shall also provide and furnish such business accommodations, apparatus and articles, and provide for the care thereof, as shall be necessary for the department of police and the transaction of the business of the police department. And the money required for such purposes, and all other sums required for the police department, shall be estimated for and raised in the manner in this act provided generally for the estimating and raising of the necessary funds for the carrying on of the work of the several departments of the city government; and such amounts as may be required from time to time by the said department shall be paid by the comptroller of said city, on the requisition of the treasurer of said department, as ordered by the board thereof, but in such sums and according to such modes and forms as shall be prescribed by the finance department, under the provision of law creating the same.

Rules and regulations. SEC. 50. The board of police are empowered, in their discretion, to enact, modify and repeal, from time to time, orders, rules and regulations of general discipline of the subordinates under their control, but in strict conformity to the provisions of this act.

Powers of police. SEC. 51. The members of the police force shall possess in the city of New York, and in every part of this state, all the common law and statutory powers of constables, except for the service of civil process, and any warrant for search or arrest, issued by any magistrate of this state, may be executed, in any part thereof, by any member of the police force, and all the provisions of sections seven, eight and nine of chapter two, title two, part four of the revised statutes, in relation to the giving and taking of bail, shall apply to this act.

Arrests to be taken at once before nearest magistrate, or stationhouse. SEC. 52. Each member of the police force, under the penalty of ten days' fine, or dismissal from the force, at the discretion of the board, shall, immediately upon an arrest, convey in person the offender before the nearest sitting magistrate, that he may be dealt with according to law. If the arrest is made during the hours that the magistrate does not regularly hold court, or if the magistrate is not holding court, such offender may be detained in a station-house or precinct thereof, until the next regular public sitting of the magistrate, and no longer, and shall then be conveyed without delay before the magistrate, to be dealt with according to law. And it shall be the duty of the said board, from time to time, to provide suitable rules and regulations to prevent the undue detention of persons arrested, which rules and regulations shall be as operative and binding as if herein specially enacted, subject, however, to the order of the court committing the person arrested. *Undue detention.*

SEC. 53. No person holding office under this department shall be liable to military or jury duty, and no officer or patrolman, while actually on duty, shall be liable to arrest on civil process, or to service of subpœna from civil courts. *Exemption from jury and military duty.*

SEC. 54. The board of police shall provide suitable accommodations for the detention of witnesses who are unable to furnish security for their appearance in criminal proceedings, to be called the house for the detention of witnesses; and such accommodation shall be in premises other than those employed for the confinement of persons charged with crime, fraud, or disorderly conduct, and be in command of a sergeant of police. And it shall be the duty of all magistrates, when committing witnesses in default of bail, to commit them to such house of detention of witnesses now or hereafter to be used for such purpose. *House of detention for witnesses.*

SEC. 55. The board of police shall have power in its *Dismissals.*

discretion, on the conviction of a member of the force of any legal offense or neglect of duty, or violation of rules, or neglect or disobedience of orders, or absence without leave, or any conduct injurious to the public peace or welfare, or immoral conduct, or conduct unbecoming an officer, or other breach of discipline, to punish the offending party by reprimand, forfeiting and withholding pay **Fines.** for a specified time, or dismissal from the force; but no more than thirty days' pay shall be forfeited for any offense. All such fines shall be paid forthwith to the treasurer of the department to the account of the police life insurance fund.

Official appointment. SEC. 56. Every member of the police force shall have issued to him by the board of police, a proper warrant of appointment, signed by the president of the said board, and chief clerk or first deputy, which warrant shall contain the date of his appointment and his rank.

Official oath. SEC. 57. Each member of the police force shall, before entering upon the duties of his office, take an oath of office, and subscribe the same before any officer of the police department who is empowered to administer an **Treasurer to give bond.** oath. The treasurer of the board of police shall give a bond, with two sureties, in the sum of twenty thousand dollars each, for the faithful performance of his duties; said bond to be approved by the comptroller and filed in his office.

SEC. 58. It shall be the duty of the superintendent of

police to detail, on each day of election, at least two patrolmen to each election poll.

Sec. 59. It shall be the duty of the police force, or any member thereof, to prevent any booth, or box, or structure for the distribution of tickets at any election from being erected or maintained within one hundred and fifty feet of any polling place within the city, and to summarily remove any such booth, box or structure, or close and prevent the use thereof.

Sec. 60. The duties of the police surgeons, and the extent and bounds of their districts, shall be assigned from time to time by the rules and regulations of the board of police.

Sec. 61. All property or money alleged or supposed to have been feloniously obtained, or which shall be lost or abandoned, and which shall be hereafter taken into the custody of any member of the police force, or criminal court of the city of New York, or which shall come into the custody of any police justice, shall be, by such member or justice, or by order of said court, given into the custody of and kept by the property clerk of the police, and all such property and money shall be particularly registered by said property clerk in a book kept for that purpose, which shall contain the name of the owner, if ascertained, the place where found, the name of the person from whom taken, with the general circumstances, the date of its receipt, the name of the officer recovering the same, the names of all claimants thereto, and any final disposition of such property or money.

Property, how returned.

SEC. 62. Whenever property or money shall be taken from persons arrested, and shall be alleged to have been feloniously obtained, or to be the proceeds of crime, and whenever so brought, with such claimant and the person arrested, before some magistrate for adjudication, and the magistrate shall be then and there satisfied from evidence that the person arrested is innocent of the offense alleged, and that the property rightfully belongs to him, then said magistrate may thereupon, in writing, order such property or money to be returned, and the property clerk, if he have it, to deliver such property or money to the accused person himself, and not to any attorney, agent or clerk of such accused person.

Claims for property to be made on oath.

SEC. 63. If any claim to the ownership of such property or money shall be made on oath before the magistrate, by or in behalf of any other persons than the person arrested, and the said accused person shall be held for trial or examination, such property or money shall remain in the custody of the property clerk until the discharge or conviction of the person accused.

Lost property to be advertised in City Record.

SEC. 64. All property or money taken on suspicion of having been feloniously obtained, or of being the proceeds of crime, and for which there is no other claimant than the person from whom such property was taken, and all lost property coming into the possession of any member of the said police force, and all property and money taken from pawnbrokers as the proceeds of crime, or by any such member from persons supposed to be insane, intoxicated or otherwise incapable of taking care of themselves, shall be transmitted, as soon as practicable, to the property clerk, to be registered and advertised in the City Record for the benefit of all persons interested, and for the information of the public, as to the amount and disposition of the property so taken into custody by the police.

SEC. 65. All property and money that shall remain in the custody of the property clerk for the period of six months without any lawful claimant thereto, after having been advertised in the City Record for the period of ten days, shall be sold at public auction in a suitable room to be designated for such purpose, and the proceeds of such sale shall be paid into the police life insurance fund. *When detained property shall be sold.*

SEC. 66. If any property or money placed in the custody of the property clerk shall be desired as evidence in any police or other criminal court, such property shall be delivered to any officer who shall present an order to that effect from such court. Such property, however, shall not be retained in said court, but shall be returned to such property clerk, to be disposed of according to the previous provisions of this act. *When property or articles may be used in court.*

SEC. 67. The board of police by this act created shall possess all the powers conferred upon the existing board of police by chapter six hundred and seventy-seven of the *Powers conferred on police board.*

laws of eighteen hundred and seventy-two, and any act or acts amendatory thereof or supplemental thereto,

Shall establish a bureau of street cleaning. except as herein otherwise provided; and shall establish in their department a bureau, which shall be called the bureau of street cleaning; the chief officer of which shall be a police officer and shall be called "inspector of street cleaning;" and who shall, under the supervision of the board of police, have charge of the cleaning of the streets,

Inspector on street cleaning. avenues and public places of the city. He shall supervise and enforce the performance of the conditions of any existing contract for such cleaning, or for the removal, under any contract now existing or hereafter made by the board of health, of night soil and contents of sinks and privies, and offal and dead animals; and shall perform such additional cleaning as, in the opinion of the board of health, is necessary to keep said streets, avenues and public places clean. He shall possess all the powers and rights imposed upon or reserved to the city inspector in any law or ordinance, or in any contract now in force, so far as the same relates to street cleaning. He shall file with the comptroller monthly a statement, under oath, showing the number of persons, and at what salary or compensation, that were employed during each day in the preceding month, and shall keep and preserve regular pay-rolls, which shall be open to reasonable public inspection.

Absence or illness of superintendent. Sec. 68. In case of the disability, absence or illness of the superintendent of police, the commissioners of police may, by resolution, designate such officer of the police force as they may choose to execute and perform the duties of the superintendent during the period of such disability, absence or illness.

SEC. 69. The police department is hereby authorized and empowered, in its name or in the name of its president or treasurer, to take and prosecute any appropriate action or proceeding in any court of record, or to continue any action heretofore commenced for such purpose, which the board of police of the metropolitan police district or its treasurer, or any other public officer or officers, but for the passage of said act, and of any other act passed since the first of January, eighteen hundred and seventy, could have taken and prosecuted, to compel the county of Richmond, or the board of supervisors of that county, or any officer of that county, to make payment of the sums due from and owing by said county of Richmond, by reason of the failure of said county and its officers to pay to the said board of metropolitan police, or the treasurer of said board of police, or into the treasury of the state, the moneys required to pay the salaries and compensation of the members of the police force of the metropolitan police district doing duty in the said county of Richmond, and defray the other lawful expenses of said police force, chargeable upon the said county of Richmond, as specified in the annual financial estimates heretofore made by the said board of metropolitan police, and all moneys that may be so collected shall

Police funds due from county of Richmond.

be paid to the chamberlain of the city of New York; the moneys so due and owing having been advanced, by the said board of metropolitan police, out of moneys raised in and contributed to the metropolitan police fund by the county of New York.

ARTICLE VIII.

Of the Department of Public Works.

Commissioner.

SEC. 70. There shall be a department of public works, the head or chief officer of which shall be called "commissioner of public works," who shall hold office for four years, and until his successor is appointed, unless sooner removed, as herein provided. Whenever the words "street commissioner" shall occur in any existing law, ordinance, resolution, contract or document, it shall be deemed to mean the aforesaid commissioner of public works, and whenever in any law, or in any ordinance of the corporation, the words "street department" shall occur, it shall be deemed and construed hereafter to mean the department of public works and the commis-

Deputy.

sioner thereof. The commissioner of public works may appoint a deputy commissioner of public works, who shall, in addition to his other powers, possess every power and perform all and every duty belonging to the office of said commissioner, whenever so empowered by said commissioner by written authority, designating therein a period of time not extending beyond the period of three months, nor beyond the term of office of the said commissioner of public works, during which said power and duty may be exercised; and such designation and authority shall be duly filed in and remain on record in the department of public works. The said deputy commissioner of public works shall possess the like authority in the case of the absence or disability of the commissioner of public works. And it shall be the duty of the commissioner to remove all obstructions now existing, or which may hereafter be placed upon any street or sidewalk, or public ground not inclosed in any public park; provided, however, that nothing contained in this section shall affect or prevent the continuance of any proceedings already commenced for assessing the expense of executing any contract made by the department of public works or the commissioner thereof.

Powers of deputy.

Powers of commissioner.

SEC. 71. The said department shall have cognizance and control—

1. Of all structures and property connected with the supply and distribution of Croton water.

2. Of the collection of the revenues arising from the sale or use of the Croton water.

3. Of opening, altering, regulating, grading, flagging, curbing, guttering, and lighting streets, roads, places and avenues.

4. Of repairing and construction of public roads.

4

5. Of the care of public buildings.

6. Of the filling of sunken lots.

7. Of public sewers and drainage.

8. Of street vaults and openings in sidewalks.

9. Of paving, repairing and repaving streets, and keeping the same clear of obstructions.*

10. Of digging and constructing wells.

Bureaus. Sec. 72. There shall be eight bureaus in the department of public works :

Water purveyor. 1. A bureau for laying water-pipes, and the construction and repair of sewers, wells and hydrants, paving and repaving and repairing streets, the chief officer of which shall be called " water purveyor."

Water register. 2. A bureau for the collection of revenue derived from the sale and use of water ; the chief officer of which shall be called " water register."

Chief engineer. 3. A bureau having care of all structures and property connected with the supply and distribution of Croton water ; the chief officer of which shall be called " chief engineer of the Croton aqueduct," with power to appoint and remove at pleasure, and detail a staff of assistant engineers. He and they must be civil engineers of at least ten years' experience. The commissioner may delegate to this bureau any power and duty now conferred by ·

* See Appendix, G.

law or ordinance on the chief engineer of the Croton aqueduct board.

4. A bureau for grading, flagging, curbing and guttering streets; the chief officer of which shall be called "superintendent of street improvements." *Superintendent of street improvements.*

5. A bureau of lamps and gas; the chief officer of which shall be called "superintendent of lamps and gas." *Superintendent of lamps and gas.*

6. A bureau of streets and roads; the chief officer of which shall be called "superintendent of streets." *Superintendent of streets.*

7. A bureau of repairs and supplies, which shall have cognizance of all supplies and repairs to public buildings, works, lands, and places, and all other repairs and supplies not provided for in other departments; the chief officer of which shall be called "superintendent of repairs and supplies," and shall be a practical builder. *Superintendent of repairs and supplies.*

8. A bureau for the removal of incumbrances on the streets or sidewalks; the chief officer of which shall be called the "superintendent of incumbrances," to whom all complaints shall be made, and by whom such incumbrances shall be removed. *Superintendent of incumbrances.*

SEC. 73. The commissioner of public works, in conjunction with the mayor and comptroller, is authorized from time to time to contract, as provided in section ninety-[one] of this act, for lighting the streets, avenues and places of the city with gas, but shall not make any arrangement or agreement with any company or com- *Contract for lighting streets.*

panies for such purpose for a period longer than one year at any given time, nor for an amount in excess of the amount appropriated therefor. The commissioner of public works is hereby authorized, in his discretion, to cause water meters, the pattern and price of which shall be approved by the mayor, comptroller, and chief engineer of the Croton aqueduct, to be placed in all stores, workshops, hotels, manufactories, public edifices, at wharves, ferry-houses, stables, and in all places in which water is furnished for business consumption by the department of public works, except private dwellings, so that all water so furnished therein or thereat may be measured and known by the said department, and for the purpose of ascertaining the ratable portion which consumers of water should pay for the water therein or thereat received and used. Thereafter, as shall be determined by the commissioner of public works, the said department shall make out all bills and charges for water furnished by them to each and every consumer as aforesaid, to whose consumption a meter as aforesaid is affixed, in ratable proportion to the water consumed, as ascertained by the meter on his or her premises or places occupied or used as aforesaid. All expenses of meters, their connections and setting, water rates, and other lawful charges for the supply of Croton water, shall be a lien upon the premises where such water is supplied as now provided by law. Nothing herein contained shall be construed so as to remit or prevent the due collection of arrearages or charges for water consumption heretofore incurred, nor

Water meters.

Water bills

Meters a lien on premises.

interfere with the proper liens therefor, nor of charges or rates, or liens hereafter to be incurred for water consumption in any dwelling-house, building or place which may not contain one of the meters aforesaid. The department of public works hereby created shall have and possess all the powers and functions heretofore or now possessed by the department of public parks, or the department of public works, in relation to the construction of the boulevard (road or public drive), streets, avenues, and roads above Fifty-ninth street, not embraced within the limits of or immediately adjacent to any park or public place; and all provisions of law conferring powers, and devolving duties upon the department of public parks, in relation thereto, are hereby transferred to and conferred upon the said department of public works.

To possess certain powers of department of parks.

ARTICLE IX.

Of the Department of Public Charities and Correction.

Sec. 74. The department of public charities and correction shall hereafter be composed of and have for its head a board of three persons, which board shall possess all the powers and discharge all the duties now conferred upon such department by special laws and by all the provisions of chapter five hundred and ten of the laws of eighteen hundred and sixty, and the acts and parts of acts amendatory thereof, except as the same are modified or repealed by the provisions of this act. The commission-

Board of charities and correction.

Their term of office.

ers, except those first appointed, shall hold office for six years, unless sooner removed as herein provided. There shall be under said commissioners a bureau of charities and a bureau of correction. The bureau of charities shall have charge of all matters relating to persons not criminals. The bureau of correction shall have charge of all matters relating to criminals.

Bureaus

SEC. 75. [*As amended by sec.* 10, *chap.* 757, *laws of* 1873.] No money belonging to the city, or city and county of New York, raised by taxation upon the property of the citizens thereof, shall be appropriated in aid of any religious or denominational school, neither shall any property, real or personal, belonging to said city, or said city and county, be disposed of to any such school, except upon the sale thereof at public auction, after the same has been duly advertised, at which sale such school shall be the highest bidder, and upon payment of the sum so bid into the city treasury, neither shall any property belonging to the city, or city and county, be leased to any school under the control of any religious or denominational institution, except upon such terms as city property may be leased to private parties after the same has been duly advertised.

Moneys, how used.

ARTICLE X.

Of the Fire Department.*

SEC. 76. The fire department shall have for its head a Fire commissioners. board, to consist of three persons to be known as fire commissioners of the city of New York, who, except those first appointed, shall hold their offices for six years, unless sooner removed as herein provided. There shall be in this department three bureaus. One bureau shall be Bureaus. charged with the duty of preventing and extinguishing fires and of protecting property from water used at fires, the principal officer of which shall be called the "chief of department." Another bureau shall be charged with the execution of all laws relating to the storage, sale and use of combustible materials, the principal officer of which shall be called "inspector of combustibles." Another bureau shall be charged with the investigation of the origin and cause of fires, the principal officer of which shall be called "fire marshal." The fire marshal shall Fire marshal. possess all the powers and perform all the duties now possessed and performed by the fire marshal, and appointed pursuant to chapter three hundred and eighty-three of the laws of eighteen hundred and seventy, and chapter five hundred and eighty-four of the laws of eighteen hundred and seventy-one, and the acts amendatory or supplementary thereof. Such fire marshal and his assistants shall hereafter be appointed by the board of

* See Appendix. H.

fire commissioners, who shall possess all the powers with reference thereto conferred by said acts upon the board of police.

Discipline, rules, orders, etc.

Sec. 77. The government and discipline of the fire department shall be such as the board may from time to time by rules, regulations, and orders prescribe; but officers and members of the uniformed force shall be removable only after written charges shall have been preferred against them, and after the charges have been publicly examined into, upon such reasonable notice. to the person charged, and in such manner of examination as the rules and regulations of the board of commissioners may prescribe. Sections forty-eight, fifty, fifty-one fifty-five, fifty-eight, sixty, sixty-one, sixty-two, of chapter one hundred and thirty-seven of the laws of eighteen hundred and seventy, are hereby made applicable to the fire department and its subordinates, so far as the same are pertinent, in the same manner as if the same were therein named.

Fines.

Any and all fines collected from subordinates shall be deposited in "the fire department relief fund" created by chapter seven hundred and forty-two of the laws of eighteen hundred and seventy-one, and the treasurer of said fund shall give a bond, with one or more sureties, in the sum of twenty thousand dollars for the faithful performance of his duties; said bond to be approved by the comptroller and filed in his office.

Membership.

Sec. 78. [*As amended by sec.* 11, *chap.* 757, *laws of* 1873.] No person shall ever be appointed to

membership in the fire department, or continue to
hold membership therein, who is not a citizen of the
United States, or who has ever been convicted of
crime, or who cannot read and write understandingly
in the English language, or who shall not have
resided within the state one year.

SEC. 79. The board of commissioners by this act created
shall possess and exercise all the powers and perform all
the duties conferred and prescribed by chapter two
hundred and forty-nine of the laws of eighteen hundred
and sixty-five, and any act or acts amendatory thereof or
supplementary thereto, not inconsistent with the provisions of this act, and except as herein otherwise provided.

General powers of board.

ARTICLE XI.

Of the Health Department.*

SEC. 80. The Health Department shall consist of the
president of the board of police, the health officer of the
port, and two officers to be called "commissioners of
health," one of whom shall have been a pratising
physician for not less than five years preceding his
appointment. The commissioner of health, who is not a
physician, shall be the president of the board, and shall
be so designated in his appointment. These several
officers shall together constitute a board, which shall be

Board of health.

* See Appendix, I.

the head of the health department. The commissioners of health, except those first appointed, shall hold their offices for six years, unless sooner removed as herein provided.

Bureaus. SEC. 81. There shall be two bureaus in this department. The chief officer of one bureau shall be called the "sanitary superintendent," who, at the time of his appointment, shall have been, for at least ten years, a practising physician and for three years a resident of the city of New York, and he shall be the chief executive officer. of said department. The chief officer of the second bureau **Record of birth, etc.** shall be called the "register of records;" and in said bureau shall be recorded, without fees, every birth, marriage and death, and all inquisitions of coroners which shall occur or be taken within the city of New York. But in cases of inquests, where the jury shall find that death was caused by negligence or malicious injury, only a copy of the record need be filed in said bureau. Said board may, with the consent of the board of police, impose any portion of the duties of subordinates in said department upon subordinates in the police department and may delegate any portion of its powers to the president or sanitary superintendent, to be exercised when the board **Board may appoint attorney.** is not in session. The said board of health may appoint an attorney at a salary not exceeding two thousand five hundred dollars a year, to be provided for and paid as other salaries in said department.

Sanitary code. SEC. 82. It shall be the duty of said board, immediately

upon organization under this act, to cause to be conformed
to this article the sanitary ordinances then or lately
adopted by the existing department of health, which shall
be called the "sanitary code." And said health department is hereby authorized and empowered to add to such
sanitary code, from time to time, and shall publish additional provisions for the security of life and health in the
city of New York, and therein to distribute appropriate
powers and duties to the members and employees of the
board of health, which shall be published in the City
Record. Any violation of said code shall be treated and Penalty for
violations.
punished as a misdemeanor, and the offender shall also be
liable to pay a penalty of fifty dollars, to be recovered in
a civil action in the name of the mayor, aldermen, and
commonalty of the city of New York. All orders duly
made by the existing department of health, and by their
terms or necessary legal effect to be executed in the city
of New York, may be executed, and the execution thereof
compelled, and the execution of such of them as are
partly executed may be compelled by the department of
health hereby created; and the said orders may be severally rescinded or modified by last said department, with
like effect as could have been done by the existing department of health at the time the said orders were severally
made. The said department may discharge all liens upon Liens.
real estate in the city of New York, created in proceedings instituted by the metropolitan board of health, or the
existing department of health, in the same manner and
for the same causes that, by laws existing January first,

eighteen hundred and seventy, they could be discharged by the metropolitan board of health.

[*Amended by adding the following—sec.* 12, *chap.* 757, *laws of* 1873.]ˑ The authority, duty and powers conferred or enjoined upon the metropolitan board of health by chapter seventy-four of the laws of eighteen hundred and sixty-six, and the several acts amendatory thereof, and by any other subsequent laws of this state, and, upon the several officers and members of said board, not inconsistent with the provisions of this act, are hereby conferred upon and vested in, or enjoined upon, and shall hereafter be exclusively exercised in the city of New York, by the health department and board of health created by this act; and by the officers of the said board of health and the said health department ; and the same are to be exercised in the manner specified in the said chapter seventy-four, of the laws of eighteen hundred and sixty-six, and the several acts amendatory thereof, and by any other subsequent laws of the state, and in conformity to the provisions of this act.

ARTICLE XII.

Of the Department of Public Parks.*

Sec. 83. [*As amended by sec.* 13, *chap.* 757, *laws of* 1873.] The department of public parks shall

* See Appendix, F, sec. 2.

control and manage all public parks and streets immediately adjoining the same above Fifty-ninth street, and public places which are the realty of the city of New York, except the buildings in the city hall park, and save as herein otherwise provided; and shall have all the powers and duties belonging to the department or commissioners of parks not inconsistent with the provisions of this act, and the laying out and preparing maps and plans of all streets, avenues and drives above Fifty-ninth street. *Powers.*

SEC. 84. [*As amended by sec.* 2, *chap.* 300, *laws of* 1874.] This department shall be under the charge of a board to consist of four members, who, except those first appointed, shall hold their offices for five years, unless sooner removed as herein provided. The office of the commissioner of parks, whose term of office expires on the first day of May, eighteen hundred and seventy-four, is hereby abolished on and after said date. The department of public parks, on and after the first day of May, eighteen hundred and seventy-four, shall be under the charge and control of four commissioners, who shall perform all the duties and exercise all the powers now by law conferred or imposed upon the department of public parks of the city of New York. *Organization of board.* *Board to consist of four commissioners.*

ARTICLE XIII.

Of the Department of Buildings.*

Superintendent of buildings.

SEC. 85. [*As amended by sec. 15, chap.* 757, *laws of* 1873.] There shall be a department called the department of buildings, which shall be under the control of an officer, who shall be known as the superintendent of buildings, and shall be the same person nominated as commissioner of buildings by the mayor of the city of New York on the fifteenth day of May, one thousand eight hundred and seventy-three, and confirmed by the board of aldermen of said city on the sixteenth day of May, one thousand eight hundred and seventy-three, which said superintendent shall hold office for the full term for which said commissioner was appointed, unless sooner removed, as provided by law for the removal of heads of departments.

Powers and duties continued.

SEC. 86. [*As amended by sec.* 15, *chap.* 757, *laws of* 1873.] Each and all the powers and duties of said department and all its officers and employees, and subordinates, and their qualifications shall continue, and be exercised as now authorized by special laws in relation to buildings in the city of New York; and it shall not be lawful for any officer or employee in said department to be engaged in conducting or

* See Appendix, J.

carrying on business as an architect, carpenter, mason, or builder, while holding office in said department.

ARTICLE XIV.

The Department of Taxes and Assessments.

SEC. 87. The department of taxes and assessments shall have for its head a president, who shall be so designated in his appointment, and two commissioners, who together shall possess all the powers and perform all the duties now possessed and performed by the commissioners of taxes and assessments. Except that it shall require a majority of such commissioners to correct or reduce the assessed valuation of the personal property of any person, and that no tax or personal property shall be remitted, canceled, or reduced, unless the applicant or party aggrieved shall satisfy the commissioners that he has been prevented by absence from the city or by illness from making his complaint or application to them within the time allowed by law for the correction of taxes. They may regulate and abolish the subordinate offices and bureaus, as shall seem most advantageous to the public service. They shall, except those first appointed, hold their offices for six years, unless sooner removed as herein provided.

ARTICLE XV.

Of the Department of Docks.

Department of docks.

SEC. 88. There shall be a department of docks, the head of which shall be a board consisting of three persons residing in the city of New York, who, except those first appointed, shall hold office for the term of six years, unless sooner removed as herein provided, and shall possess such powers and perform such duties as are now possessed by the existing department of docks, but said

Exterior line.

board shall not have the power to change the exterior line of piers and bulk-heads in the city of New York as now established by law.

ARTICLE XVI.

General Provisions, Powers, and Limitations.

Quorum.

SEC. 89. A majority of the members of a board in any department of the city government, and also of the board for the revision and correction of assessments, shall constitute a quorum to fully perform and discharge any act or duty authorized, possessed by, or imposed upon any department or any board aforesaid, and with the same legal effect as if every member of any such board aforesaid had been present, except as herein otherwise

Officers.

specially provided. Each board may, except as herein otherwise provided, choose, in its own pleasure, one of its members, who shall be its president, and one who shall be its treasurer, and may appoint a chief clerk or secretary. No expense shall be incurred by any of the departments, boards, or officers thereof, unless an appropriation shall have been previously made covering such expense.

How expenses may be incurred.

SEC. 90. Whatever provisions and regulations, other than those herein specially authorized, may become requisite for the fuller organization, perfecting, and carrying out of the powers and duties prescribed to any department by this act, shall be provided for by ordinance of the common council, who are hereby authorized to enact such necessary ordinances. And it shall be the duty of the common council to provide for the accountability of all officers and other persons, save as herein otherwise provided, to whom the receipt or expenditure of the funds of the city shall be intrusted, by requiring from them sufficient security for the performance of their duties or trust, which security shall be annually renewed; but the security first taken shall remain in force until new security shall be given.

Full powers given to common council.

Officers intrusted with funds to give security.

SEC. 91. All contracts to be made or let for work to be done, or supplies to be furnished, except as herein otherwise provided, and all sales of personal property in the custody of the several departments or bureaus, shall be made by the appropriate heads of departments under such regulations as now exist or shall be established by ordinances of the common council. Whenever any work is necessary to be done to complete or perfect a particular job, or any supply is needful for any particular purpose,

Contracts.

Work to be done under contracts.

5

which work and job is to be undertaken or supply furnished for the corporation, and the several parts of the said work or supply shall together involve the expenditure of more than one thousand dollars, the same shall be by contract, under such regulations concerning it as shall be established by ordinance of the common council, excepting such works now in progress as are authorized by law or ordinance to be done otherwise than by contract; and unless otherwise ordered by a vote of three-fourths of the members elected to the common council; and all contracts shall be entered into by the appropriate heads of departments, and shall, except as herein otherwise provided, be founded on sealed bids or proposals, made in compliance with public notice duly advertised in the City Record, said notice to be published at least ten days; and all such contracts, when given, shall be given to the lowest bidder, the terms of whose contracts shall be settled by the counsel to the corporation as an act of preliminary specification to the bid or proposal, and who shall give security for the faithful performance of his contract in the manner prescribed and required by ordinance; and the adequacy and sufficiency of this security shall, in addition to the justification and acknowledgment, be approved by the comptroller. All bids or proposals shall be publicly opened by the officers advertising for the same and in the presence of the comptroller, but the opening of the bids shall not be postponed if the comptroller shall, after due notice, fail to attend. If the lowest bidder shall neglect or refuse to accept to contract within forty-eight hours

Proposals to be advertised.

Contractor to give security.

Bids to be publicly opened.

Neglect to ratify an accepted bid.

after written notice that the same has been awarded to his
bid or proposal, or if he accepts but does not execute the
contract and give the proper security, it shall be re-advertised and relet as above provided. In case any work shall
be abandoned by any contractor, it shall be re-advertised
and relet by the head of the appropriate department, in
the manner in this section provided.

SEC. 92. All property sold shall be sold at auction, after *Property to be sold at auction.*
previous public notice, under the superintendence of the
appropriate head of department. Every contract, when *Contracts to be filed in duplicate.*
made and entered into, as before provided for, shall be
executed in duplicate, and shall be filed in the department
of finance; a receipt for each payment, made on account
of or in satisfaction of the same, shall be indorsed on the
said contract by the party receiving the warrant, which
warrant shall be only given to the person interested in
such contract, or his authorized representative. The pro- *Proceeds of sales.*
ceeds of all sales made under and by virtue of this act
shall, except as provided in section sixty-five hereof, be
by the officer receiving the same immediately deposited
with the chamberlain; and the account of sales, verified
by the officer making the sales, shall be immediately filed
in the office of the comptroller. No expenditure for
work or supplies involving an amount for which no contract is required shall be made, except the necessity
therefor be certified to by the head of the appropriate
department, and the expenditure has been duly authorized
and appropriated.

Certificate of office.

SEC. 93. Every person who shall be appointed or elected to any office under this act shall receive a certificate of appointment, designating the term for which such person has been appointed or elected.

Oath to be taken by all officers.

SEC. 94. Every person elected or appointed to any office under the city government shall, within five days after notice of such election or appointment, take and subscribe, before the mayor, or any judge of a court of record, an oath or affirmation faithfully to perform the duties of his office; which oath or affirmation shall be filed in the office of the mayor.

Violations of this act, how punished.

SEC. 95. Any officer of the city government, or person employed in its service, who shall willfully violate or evade any of the provisions of this act, or commit any fraud upon the city, or convert any of the public property to his own use, or knowingly permit any other person so to convert it, or by gross or culpable neglect of duty allow the same to be lost to the city, shall be deemed guilty of a misdemeanor, and, in addition to the penalties imposed by law, and on conviction, shall forfeit his office, and be excluded forever after from receiving or holding any office under the city government; and any person who shall willfully swear falsely in any oath or affirmation required by this act shall be guilty of perjury.

SEC. 96. [*As amended by sec. 16, chap.* 757, *laws of* 1873.] No officer of the city government, except the city marshals, shall have or receive to his own use

Salary in lieu of fees, perquisites, etc.

any fees, perquisites, or commissions, or any percentage; but every such officer shall be paid by a fixed salary, and all fees, percentages and commissions received by any such officer shall be the property of the city. And every officer who shall receive any fees, perquisites, commissions, percentages or other money which should be paid over to the city, shall, before he shall be entitled to receive any salary, make under oath a detailed return to the comptroller, showing the amount of all such fees, commissions, percentages, perquisites and moneys received by him since the last preceding report, the person from whom received, and the reason for its payment, and shall produce the receipt of the chamberlain, showing the payment to him, by said officer, of the aggregate amount thereof. All sums received as above or for licenses or permits shall be paid over weekly, without deduction, by the officers or department receiving them, to the chamberlain, and a detailed return under oath shall at the same time be made in such form as the comptroller shall prescribe, stating when and from whom, and for what use, such moneys were received. But nothing herein contained shall be construed so as to repeal, modify, or otherwise affect the provisions of the fourteenth section of chapter seven hundred and forty-two of the laws of eighteen hundred and seventy-one.

Fees, etc., to be paid over weekly.

Salaries, how fixed.

SEC. 97. The salaries of all officers paid from the city treasury, whose offices now exist but are not embraced in any department, shall be fixed by the board of apportionment. Such board may, by a majority vote, reduce any such salaries, but shall not increase the salary of any office the compensation of which now exceeds three thousand dollars.

When salaries shall be prescribed by ordinance.

SEC. 98. The salaries of all officers, whose offices may be created by the common council for the purpose of giving effect to the provisions of this act, shall be prescribed by ordinance or resolution, to be passed by the common council, and approved as hereinbefore provided for the approval of ordinances or resolutions.

Bidder in arrears.

SEC. 99. No bid shall be accepted from, or contract awarded to, any person who is in arrears to the corporation upon debt or contract, or who is a defaulter, as surety or otherwise, upon any obligation to the corporation.

Bribery, in any form, to be deemed felony.

SEC. 100. Every person who shall promise, offer, or give, or cause, or aid, or abet in causing to be promised, offered, or given, or furnish or agree to furnish, in whole or in part, to any other person, to be promised, offered or given, to any member of the common council, or any officer of the corporation, or clerk, after his election or appointment as such officer, member, or clerk, or before or after he shall have qualified and taken his seat, or entered upon his duty, any moneys, goods, right in action or other property, or anything of value, or any pecuniary advan-

tage, present or prospective, with intent to influence his
vote, opinion, judgment or action on any question, matter,
cause or proceedings which may be then pending, or may
by law be at any time brought before him in his official
or clerical capacity, shall be deemed guilty of a felony,
and shall, upon conviction, be imprisoned in a peniten- *How punished.*
tiary for a term not exceeding two years, or shall be fined
not exceeding five thousand dollars, or both, in the discretion of the court. Every officer in this section enumer-
ated, who shall accept any such gift or promise, or under-
taking to make the same under any agreement or under-
standing that his vote, opinion, judgment or action shall
be influenced thereby, or shall be given in any question,
matter, cause or proceeding then or at any time pending,
or which may by law be brought before him in his official
capacity, shall be deemed guilty of a felony, and shall,
upon conviction, be disqualified from holding any public
office, trust or appointment under the city of New York,
and shall forfeit his office, and shall be punished by imprisonment in the penitentiary not exceeding two years, or
by a fine not exceeding five thousand dollars, or both, in
the discretion of the court. Every person offending *Offenders
competent
witnesses.*
against either of the provisions of this section shall be
a competent witness against any other person offending
in the same transaction, and may be compelled to appear
and give evidence before any grand jury, or in any court,
in the same manner as other persons; but the testimony so
given shall not be used in any prosecution or proceeding,
civil or criminal, against the person so testifying.

SEC. 101. No member of the common council, head of department, chief of bureau, deputy thereof, or clerk therein, or other officer of the corporation, shall be or become, directly or indirectly, interested in or in the performance of any contract, work or business, or the sale of any article, the expense, price or consideration of which is payable from the city treasury, or by any assessment levied by any act or ordinance of the common council; nor in the purchase or lease of any real estate or other property belonging to or taken by the corporation, or which shall be sold for taxes or assessments, or by virtue of legal process at the suit of the said corporation. If any person in this section mentioned shall, during the time for which he was elected or appointed, knowingly acquire an interest in any contract or work with the city, or any department or officer thereof, unless the same shall be devolved upon him by law, he shall, on conviction thereof, forfeit his office, and be punished as for a misdemeanor. All such contracts in which any such person is or becomes interested shall, at the option of the comptroller, be forfeited and void. No person in this section named shall give or promise to give any portion of his compensation or any money or valuable thing to any officer of the city, or to any other person, in consideration of his having been or being nominated, appointed, elected or employed as such officer, agent, clerk or employee, under the penalty of forfeiting his office and being forever disqualified from being elected, appointed,

Marginal notes:
Corporation officers not to be interested in contracts.

Penalty.

When contract shall be declared void.

or employed in the service of the city, and shall, on conviction, be punished for a misdemeanor.

SEC. 102. [*As amended by sec.* 17, *chap.* 757, *laws of* 1873.] There shall continue to be, as now provided and recognized by special laws and ordinances, a board of commissioners of the sinking fund composed of the mayor, recorder, chamberlain, comptroller, and the chairman of the finance committee of the board of aldermen, with all the powers and duties now assigned, designated and ratified by existing laws and ordinances. The said board shall have power to sell or lease, for the highest marketable price or rental, at public auction or by sealed bids, and always after public advertisement and appraisal under the direction of said board, any city property, except wharves and piers. But if said property be market property, excepting the market between Sixteenth and Seventeenth streets, east of avenue " C," the market in Gouverneur slip, and the market in Old slip, it shall not be sold or leased unless under a condition that the purchaser or lessee thereof shall maintain said market property as and for the purposes of a public market, for at least ten years from and after such sale or lease, and under due ordinances of the common council or of the department of health, or under stipulations in the deed of sale or lease. The proceeds of said sale or leasing shall, on receipt thereof, after paying necessary

[Marginal notes:] Commissioners of the sinking fund. — Have power to sell or lease property. — Market property. — Proceeds of sale.

charges, be immediately paid to the credit of the sinking fund. It shall be lawful for the commissioners of the sinking fund of the city of New York, in their discretion, and they are hereby empowered in such discretion to cancel any portion of the indebtedness of the said city held by them, which is by law redeemable from the sinking fund, and to sell any stocks and bonds which they may hold that are not payable from said fund, and with the proceeds of such sale of stocks and bonds to buy any other stocks and bonds which are payable from said fund.

SEC. 103. [*Repealed by sec. 18, chap. 757, laws of* 1873.]

Election laws, how applied.

SEC. 104. All the provisions of law now in force in regard to the duration, manner of conducting elections, and canvass, estimate and disposition of votes at general elections shall apply to each election of city officers.

Board of street opening, powers of.

SEC. 105. The mayor, comptroller, commissioner of public works, the president of the department of public parks, and the president of the board of aldermen, shall hereafter together form a board to be known as "the board of street opening and improvement," in place and stead of the board of street openings heretofore constituted by law ; shall keep full records of its proceedings, and shall have all the powers and authority as to laying out, opening, widening, straightening, extending, altering and closing streets or avenues, or parts of streets or avenues, in that part of the city of New York south

of Fifty-ninth street, now in any manner otherwise
conferred and vested by any other law or provision
thereof, or under existing laws which relate to altering the map or plan of said city; and the said board
are hereby authorized and empowered, whenever they
may deem it for public interest so to do, after laying
its proposed action before the board of aldermen, and
publishing full notice of the same for ten days in the
City Record herein provided for, to alter the map or plan
of New York city so as to lay out new streets in said part
of said city, and from time to time to cause maps, showing the several streets or avenues so laid out, opened,
widened, straightened, extended, altered or closed by
them, to be certified by them and filed, one in the office
of the department of public works of said city, and one in
the office of the counsel to the corporation of said city, and
it shall be the duty of the said counsel to the corporation,
on the filing of said maps in his office, together with a
requisition in writing of said board, immediately to take
proceedings, in the name of the mayor, aldermen and
commonalty of said city, to acquire title for the use of the
public to the land required for the streets or avenues so
laid out, opened, widened, straightened, extended or
altered, and for that purpose to make application to the
supreme court in the first judicial district, and in such
manner as the said board shall direct, for the appointment
of commissioners of estimate and assessment, indicating
in such application the land required for that purpose by
reference to said maps on file as aforesaid; and the pro-

Notices to
lay out new
streets to be
published.

76

Proceedings to acquire title.

ceedings to acquire title to such lands shall be had pursuant to such acts as shall be then in force relative to the opening, straightening, extending, widening or altering streets, roads, avenues and public squares and places in the city of New York, which said acts, so far as the same are not inconsistent with the provisions of this section, are hereby made applicable to the streets and avenues, or parts of streets and avenues, so laid out, opened, widened, straightened, extended and altered, and to the proceedings authorized hereby, except that the commissioners of estimate and assessment who may be appointed by the supreme court for acquiring title to any land required for the purposes of this section may assess therefor all such lands and tenements as they may deem to be benefited by such improvement, and to the extent and amount which they may deem such lands and tenements benefited thereby; and the said board is also

Closing of streets.

authorized and empowered to close all such streets and avenues, or such parts thereof as they may deem for the public interest so to do, and to direct the said counsel to the corporation to take such proceedings in the name of the mayor, aldermen and commonalty for the closing of such streets or avenues, or parts thereof, as are now or shall be then provided by law, who shall thereupon apply to the supreme court for the appointment of commissioners of estimate and assessment in the matter of the closing of said street, avenue or part thereof in the manner provided by law. And said board is also authorized and

When legal proceedings as to streets may be discontinued.

empowered to discontinue any and all legal proceedings

taken for laying out, opening, widening, straightening, extending, altering or closing streets or avenues, or parts of streets or avenues, south of Fifty-ninth street, under this act, at any time before the confirmation of the report of the commissioners of estimate and assessment in such proceedings, if in the opinion of said board the public interest requires such discontinuance, and with power to cause new proceedings to be taken in such cases for the appointment of new commissioners. A majority of said Quorum of board shall constitute a quorum, but the vote of a majority of all the members thereof shall be necessary to any act of said board. The comptroller of the city of New York, is authorized to borrow, from time to time, on the credit of the corporation, in anticipation of its revenues, and not to exceed in amount the amount of such revenues, such sums as may be necessary to meet expenditures under the appropriations for each current year. No action shall Actions on claims. be maintained against the mayor, aldermen and commonalty of the city of New York, unless the claim on which the action is brought has been presented to the comptroller, and he has neglected for thirty days after such presentment to pay the same. Before any execution shall be Notice to comptroller of judgments. issued on any judgment recovered upon such a claim, a notice of the recovery thereof shall also be given to the comptroller, and he shall be allowed ten days to provide for its payment by the issue of revenue bonds in the usual manner according to law.

Sec. 106. The mayor shall, from time to time, appoint

and remove at pleasure two persons, who, together with the president of the department of taxes and assessments, shall be commissioners of accounts. It shall be their duty, once in three months, and oftener if they deem it proper, to examine all vouchers and accounts in the offices of the comptroller and chamberlain, and to make and publish, in the City Record, a detailed statement of the financial condition of the city, showing the amount of its funded and floating debt, the amount received and expended since the last preceding report, with a classification of the sources of revenue and expenditure, and such

other information as they shall deem proper. They shall from time to time make an examination of the expenses of the several departments and officers, and make such recommendations to the board of apportionment, and other officers, with reference thereto, and particularly with reference to salaries and duties, as they deem advisable.

Any one of such commissioners shall have authority at any time to make any such examination, and such two appointed commissioners shall be paid a reasonable compensation, to be fixed as other expenditures by the board of apportionment, not exceeding three thousand dollars each annually.

SEC. 107. The heads of all departments, except the police department, and the chiefs of each and every bureau of said departments, or any of them, except the police department, shall, with reasonable promptness, furnish to any taxpayer desiring the same a true and certified copy of any book, account or paper kept by such Books open to the public. department, bureau, or officer, or such part thereof as may be demanded, upon payment in advance of five cents for every hundred words thereof by the person demanding the same. All books, accounts and papers, in any department or bureau thereof, except the police department, shall at all times be open to the inspection of any taxpayer, subject to any reasonable rules and regulations in regard to the time and manner of such inspection as such department, bureau or officer may make in regard to the same, in order to secure the safety of such books, accounts and papers, and the proper use of them by the department, bureau or officer. In case such inspection shall be Order of court in case of refusal to inspect books. refused, such taxpayer, on his sworn petition, describing the particular book, account or paper that he desires to inspect, may, upon notice of not less than one day to such department, bureau or officer, apply to any justice of the supreme court for an order that he be allowed to make such inspection as such justice shall by his order authorize, and such order shall specify the time and manner of such inspection.

SEC. 108. It shall be the duty of the comptroller to Financial statement to be published in City Record. publish in the City Record, two months before the election of charter officers, a full and detailed statement of the receipts and expenditures of the corporation during the year ending on the first day of the month in which such publication is made, and the cash balance or surplus; and in every such statement the different sources of city revenue, and the amount received from each, the several appropriations made, the objects for which the same were made, and the amount of moneys expended under each, the moneys borrowed on the credit of the corporation, the authority under which each loan was made, and the terms on which the same was obtained, shall be clearly and particularly specified.

SEC. 109. Any alderman, commissioner, head of department, chief of bureau, deputy thereof, or clerk therein, or other officer of the corporation or person, may, if a judge shall so order, be summarily examined upon an order to be made on application based on an affidavit of the mayor or of the comptroller, or any five aldermen, or any commissioners of accounts, or of any five citizens who are taxpayers, requiring such examination, and signed by any justice of the supreme court of the first judicial department, directing such examination to be publicly made at the chambers of said court, or at the office of said department, on a day and hour to be named, not less, however, than forty-eight hours after personal service of said order. Such examination shall be confined to an inquiry into any alleged wrongful diversion or misapplication of any moneys or fund, or any violation of the provisions of law, or any want of mechanical qualification for any inspectorship of public work, or any neglect of duty in acting as such inspector, or any delinquency charged in said affidavit touching the office or the discharge or neglect of duty, of which it is alleged in the application for said order that such alderman, head of department, or other aforementioned officer or persons, has knowledge or information. Such alderman, commissioner, head of department, clerk, or other aforesaid officer or person shall answer such pertinent questions relative thereto, and produce such books and papers in his custody, or under his control, as the justice shall direct, and the examination may be continued from time to time, as such justice may order, but the answer of the party charged shall not be used against him in any criminal proceeding ; provided, however, that for all false answers on material points he shall be subject to the pains and penalties of the crime of perjury. The proceedings may be continued before any other justice in said district, and other witnesses, as well as the parties making such application, may, in the discretion of said justice, be compelled to attend and be examined touching such alleged delinquencies. Such justice may punish any refusal to attend such examination or to answer any questions pursuant to his order, as for a contempt of court, and shall have as full power and authority to enforce obedience to the order or directions of himself, or any other justice, as any justice of the supreme court may now have, or shall possess, to enforce obedience or to punish contempt in any case or matter whatever, and shall impose costs upon those promoting such an examination not exceeding two hundred and fifty dollars, if he thinks there was no probable cause for making the application hereinbefore provided for, the said costs to be paid

Books and papers may be produced in court.

Witnesses may be examined.

Powers of justice.

Costs, how imposed.

6

to the officer or person examined, and for which the said officer or person may have judgment and an execution.

Examination to be filed. The examination hereinbefore provided for shall be reduced to writing, and be filed in the office of the county clerk of the county of New York, and be at all reasonable times accessible to the public, and notice of the same given to the department in which said officer is employed.

Weekly abstract of business of departments to be published. SEC. 110. In every department or board there shall be kept a record of all its transactions, which shall be accessible to the public, and once a week a brief abstract, omitting formal language, shall be made of all transactions, and of all contracts awarded and entered into for work and material of every description, which abstract shall contain the name or names, and residences by street and number, of the party or parties to the contract, and of their sureties, if any. A copy of such abstract shall be promptly transmitted to the person designated to prepare the City Record, and shall be published therein. **Appointments and removals to be published.** Notice of all appointments and removals from office, and all changes of salaries, shall, in like manner, within one week after they are made, be transmitted to and published in the City Record.

City Record. SEC. 111. There shall be published daily (Sundays and legal holidays excepted), under a contract to be made as hereinafter provided, a paper to be known as the "City Record." The mayor, corporation counsel and commissioner of public works shall appoint a proper person, together with such assistants as may be required to supervise the preparation and publication of the same, and they shall also fix the rates of compensation of said supervisor and his assistants. All the expenses connected with its publication and distribution, except the salary of the person appointed to supervise the same, and the salaries of his assistants, shall be covered by a contract for printing, to be made in the same manner as other contracts. The board of estimate and apportionment shall provide for all the necessary expenses of establishing and conducting the said City Record. There shall be inserted in said City Record nothing aside from such official matters as are in this act expressly authorized. The contract for the publication of the City Record shall provide for furnishing, free of charge, to the city not more than one thousand copies thereof, also for a gratuitous distribution to every newspaper regularly printed in the city of New York, when it shall apply for the same, of two copies, and to every public library or public institution in said city which shall apply for the same, of one copy. Copies of the same shall be sold by the publisher at a price to be fixed by the officers making the contract, and the proceeds thereof shall be paid over to the city. All advertising required to be done for the city, and all notices required by law or ordinance to be published in corporation papers, shall be inserted, at the public expense, only in the City Record, and a publication therein shall be a sufficient compliance with any law or ordinance requiring publication of such matters or notices; but there may be

Expenses of publishing.

Contract.

Sale of City Record.

Advertising.

Advertisements in other papers. inserted in two morning and two evening and two weekly papers published in the English language, and in one newspaper published in the German language, all in said city, to be designated by the mayor, corporation counsel and commissioner of public works, annually, brief advertisements calling attention to any contracts intended to be awarded, or bonds to be sold, and referring for full information to said City Record. No money shall be paid from the city treasury for advertising hereafter done except such as is herein authorized, and no action shall be maintained or judgment obtained against the city for any advertising hereafter done except such as is herein authorized. The copies of the City Record furnished to the city shall be distributed to the several departments and officers, and to such persons and in such manner as the mayor shall direct. All printing for said city, including the printing of the City Record, shall be executed, and all stationery shall be supplied, under contracts, to be entered into by the mayor, corporation counsel and commissioner of public works. The first contract for printing the City Record shall be awarded after an advertisement in the five daily newspapers printed in said city having the largest circulation therein, for at least two weeks, inviting proposals. All proposals for printing and stationery shall be based upon specifications to be filed in the department of public works, which shall set forth with accuracy the number of every description of printed blanks; also each description of stationery or blank books in ordinary use in the board of aldermen and the respective departments,

Contract for printing City Record.

Stationery and blanks.

and likely to be required during the year for which such contract is to be given; and the bids shall be given for such number of each printed description of blanks, or of each article of stationery (including under the head of stationery, letter or writing paper, or envelopes, with printed headings or indorsements) as are specified, and for such additional number as may be required, giving the price for blanks of every description, and the price of all other printing "per thousand ems," or for "rule and figure work;" separate contracts shall be made with the lowest bidder for any one description of printing, or any article of stationery involving an expense of more than five hundred dollars. Ten per cent. of the amount becoming due, from time to time, shall be withheld by the comptroller until the completion of the contract; and in case the contractor shall fail to fulfill the same to the satisfaction of the mayor, corporation counsel and commissioner of public works, then they may declare said contract to be annulled, and they shall immediately give notice for other bids for such printing during the remainder of the term of contract. No judgment shall be recovered against the city for printing or stationery done or furnished after the passage of this act, unless done or furnished under a contract where, under the provisions of this act, a contract is necessary, or under a valid contract or a contract now in force, or unless upon evidence of a contract made as provided in this section. Separate contracts may be made at any time for engraving, lithographing, woodcuts, maps or other picture work, as the same may be required; but

Ten per cent. on contract to be withheld.

Separate contracts for engravings, maps, etc.

nothing herein contained shall be construed to require a separate contract for each engraving, lithograph or wood-cut or map, unless the officers aforesaid shall deem the same advisable for the interest of the city. No more than one thousand copies of any message of the mayor, or report of any head of a department, and no more than five hundred copies of any report of a committee of the board of aldermen, or board of assistant aldermen, shall be printed apart from the City Record. Neither the work known as the Manual of the Common Council nor any similar work shall be printed at the public expense; but there shall be published in the City Record, within the month of January in each year, a list of all subordinates employed in any department (except laborers), with their salaries, and residences by street numbers, and all changes in such subordinates or salaries shall be so published within one week after they are made. It shall be the duty of all heads of departments to furnish, to the person appointed to supervise the publication of the City Record, everything required to be inserted therein. The said person shall have the power to make requisitions in writing upon the heads of departments to furnish the information necessary to make up such list according to rules prescribed by him and approved by the comptroller; and such information must be supplied by the department within ten days after such requisition. He shall have power to require such information in the same manner, every three months, and all other information in the control of said heads of departments, necessary to perform

Copies of messages and reports limited.

City Manual.

List of all officers and subordinates to be published yearly

Powers of supervisor of City Record.

his duties under this section. He shall include in his list the number of laborers, designating the department in which they are employed, and, if practicable, the numbers employed in the prosecution of specific work, and the amounts paid to them. He shall also cause to be printed in each issue of said City Record a separate statement of the hours during which all public offices in the city are open for business, and at which each court regularly opens and adjourns, as well as of the places where such offices are kept and such courts are held. The detailed canvass of votes at every election shall be published at the expense of the city only in the City Record. The mayor may order the insertion of any official matter or report in the City Record.

Official hours for business of all departments to be published daily.

Election canvass.

[*Amended by adding the following—sec.* 1, *chap.* 631, *laws of* 1875.] Nothing herein contained shall apply to any printing or supplies of stationery for the mayor, aldermen, and commonalty of the city of New York, where, by the concurrent vote of the mayor, counsel to the corporation, and the commissioner of public works, it shall be decided to have such printing done or such stationery furnished without contract let after advertisements for bids or proposals; but in such cases such printing shall be done and such stationery procured in the manner, and on such terms and conditions as the said officers shall deem to be for the best interests of the city.*

When printing and supplies may be furnished without contract.

* See Appendix, K.

SEC. 112. [*As amended by sec.* 20, *chap.* 757, *laws of* 1873.] The mayor, comptroller, president of the board of aldermen, and the president of the department of taxes and assessments, shall constitute a board of estimate and apportionment, who shall, annually, between the first day of August and the first day of November, meet, and, by the affirmative vote of all the members, make a provisional estimate of the amounts required to pay the expenses of conducting the public business of the city and county of New York, in each department and branch thereof, and the board of education for the then next ensuing financial year. In such provisional estimate they shall include such sum as may be necessary for the payment of the interest on the bonds of the said city and county, which shall become due and payable within said year, and such sum as shall be necessary to pay the principal of any bonds and stocks which may become due and payable from taxes during said year, and also so much as may be necessary to pay the proportion of the state tax required to be paid by the city and county of New York in said year. Such provisional estimate shall be prepared in such detail as to the aggregate sum allowed to each department and bureau as the said board of apportionment shall deem advisable. For the purpose of making said provisional estimate, the heads of departments and the board of education shall, at least thirty days before the said provisional estimate is required to be

Board of estimate and apportionment.

Provisional estimate.

Provisional estimate, what to contain.

Estimates in detail.

Heads of departments to furnish statement.

made as herein provided, send to the board of apportionment an estimate in writing, herein called a departmental estimate, of the amount of expenditure, specifying in detail the objects thereof, required in their respective departments, including a statement of each of the salaries of their officers, clerks, employees and subordinates. The same statement as to salaries and expenditure shall be made by all other officers, persons and boards having power to fix or authorize them. A duplicate of these departmental estimates and statements shall be made at the same time to the board of aldermen. The board of apportionment shall consider such departmental estimates and other statements in making the provisional estimates herein provided, and in approving the salaries of the officers, clerks and other persons before named. After such provisional estimate is made by the board of apportionment, it shall be submitted by said board, with their reasons for it in detail, within ten days, to the board of aldermen, whereupon a special meeting of said board shall be called to consider such estimate, and the same shall simultaneously be published in the City Record; and it shall be their duty carefully to consider and investigate the said provisional estimate and the reasons assigned therefor; but such consideration and investigation shall not continue beyond fifteen days. Any objections to or rectifications of said provisional estimate made by said board of aldermen shall be

Duplicate estimate submitted to board of aldermen.

Corrections may be made.

made by said board in writing, and transmitted by
the clerk thereof to the board of apportionment, who
shall proceed to the consideration of such objections
or rectifications, and after such consideration shall
make a final estimate. Should the said board over-
rule the objections or suggestions made by the board
of aldermen, the reasons for such action shall be
published in the City Record. After the final estimate is made, in accordance herewith, it shall be
signed by the members, and when so signed the said
several sums shall be and become appropriated to
the several purposes and departments therein named.
The said estimate shall be filed in the office of the
comptroller and published in the City Record. The
aggregate amount so estimated shall be certified by
the comptroller to the supervisors of the county of
New York; and it shall be the duty of said supervisors, and they are hereby empowered and directed
annually to cause to be raised, according to law, and
collected by tax upon the estates, real and personal,
subject to taxation within the city and county of New
York, the said amounts so estimated and certified as
aforesaid. The first meeting of said board in every
year shall be called by notice from the mayor, personally served upon the members of said board.
Subsequent meetings shall be called as the said board
shall direct. At such meetings the mayor shall preside, and one of the number shall act as secretary.
In addition to the estimate herein provided for, the

Final estimate to be signed and filed.

Supervisors to meet and consider such estimate, and raise the same by tax.

Meetings of supervisors.

said board may, at any time, as occasion may require, by the affirmative vote of three members, authorize the issue of any stocks or bonds for the purpose of withdrawing or taking up at maturity any stocks or bonds for the purpose outstanding; but the said bonds or their proceeds shall be applied exclusively to the payment, purchase and extinction of such maturing bonds in such manner that the aggregate of the stocks or bonds of said city outstanding shall not be increased thereby for a longer period than is necessary in effecting said change. The said board of apportionment may, from time to time, by the affirmative vote of three members, authorize the issue of the whole or any portion of any stock or bonds which are now by law authorized to be issued, upon compliance with the provisions of law authorizing them. The said board of apportionment may, from time to time, on the application of the head of any department, authorize the transfer, from one bureau or purpose to another in the same department, of any sum theretofore appropriated for the purpose of such department or bureau, but no department or officer shall incur any expense in excess of sum appropriated. The board of apportionment may, within forty days after the passage hereof, revise and readjust, in accordance with the provisions hereof, the apportionment heretofore made. All the provisions of law creating any board of apportionment and audit, or either, and providing

May author ize issue of stocks or bonds.

Appropriations, how transferred.

Repeal of certain provisions.

for and requiring an audit and allowance of claims by said board, are hereby repealed; but such repeal shall not, prior to the organization of the board of apportionment by this act created, affect any act heretofore done or directed to be done; but all the powers now possessed by any such board, not inconsistent with the provisions of this act, are hereby continued and vested in the board hereby created and authorized, and all actions or proceedings in which the mayor, aldermen and commonalty of the city of New York are plaintiffs or defendants, shall have a preference, and may be moved out of their *Unexpended balances.* order on the calendar. Any balances of appropriations remaining unexpended, after allowing sufficient to satisfy all claims payable therefrom, may at any time, after the expiration of the year for which they were made, be transferred by the comptroller, with the approval of said board of estimate and apportionment, to the general fund of the city, and applied to the reduction of taxation.

Unexpended appropriations may be transferred. [*As amended by sec. 2, chap. 308, laws of* 1874.] The said board of estimate and apportionment shall have the power at any time to transfer any appropriation for any year which may be found, by the head of the department for which such appropriation shall have been made, to be in excess of the amount required or deemed to be necessary for the purposes or objects thereof, to such other purposes or objects for which the appropriations are insufficient, or such as may require the same; and if it is found at the time when the estimate is made of the expenses of conducting the public business of the city of New York for the next succeeding fiscal year, that there will be a surplus or balance remaining unexpended of any appropriation then existing at the end of the current fiscal year, such surplus may be applied to like purposes in the next succeeding year.*

SEC. 113. No appropriation or payment for the contesting of the office of mayor, or any seat in the board of aldermen, or office in any department, or the office of any officer whose salary is paid from the city treasury, shall be made to any but the prevailing party. Nor shall any such appropriation or payment be made to such prevailing party, except upon the written certificates of the chief officer of the law department and of the chief justice of the court of common pleas of the city and county of New York, as to the value of the services rendered in the case. In case an officer or clerk is ordered to be examined, in pursuance of the provisions hereinbefore contained, the law department shall assign some one from his department as counsel to the officer or clerk making the application, but should such officer or clerk see fit to employ other counsel than that assigned by the law department, then, and in that event, no appropriation or payment shall be made for his or their

Contesting elections, costs of, how paid.

Counsel in case of examination of officer or clerk.

See Appendix, L, M, and N.

payment except upon a certificate of the justice or justices before whom the proceedings have been had that there was probable cause for taking such proceedings.

City officers not to hold state or federal office ;

SEC. 114. Any person holding office, whether by election or appointment, who shall, during his term of office, accept, hold, or retain any other civil office of honor, trust, or emolument under the government of the United States (except commissioners for the taking of bail, or register of any court), or of the State (except the office of notary public or commissioner of deeds, or office of the national guard), or who shall hold or accept any other office connected with the government of the city of New York, or who shall accept a seat in the legislature, shall be deemed thereby to have vacated every office held by him under the city government. No person shall hold two city or

nor more than city or county office.

county offices, except as expressly provided in this act; nor shall any officer under the city government hold or retain an office under the county government, except when he holds such office ex-officio, by virtue of an act of the legislature; and in such case he shall draw no salary for such ex-officio office.

Consulting engineers.

[*Amended by adding the following—sec.* 21, *chap.* 757, *laws of* 1873.] This section shall not be construed to apply to civil or consulting engineers who may be appointed to superintend any specific work, on the part of the city of New York.

SEC. 115. [*As amended by sec.* 1, *chap.* 476, *laws*

of 1875.] Whenever the commissioner of public works of the city of New York shall certify and report to the board of aldermen of said city that the safety, health, or convenience of the public requires the re-pavement of any streets, avenues, or public places in said city, said board of aldermen shall have the power to direct by ordinance or resolution, the repavement of said streets, avenues, or public places, in the man-ner specified and of the materials approved of and recommended by said commissioner of public works, which work shall be done by and under the direction of the department of public works, according to law. In case any of the streets, avenues, or public places in said city shall have been once paved, and the ex-pense thereof assessed upon the owners of adjoining and benefited property, the cost of the repaving thereof shall be borne by a general assessment upon all taxable property in said city. The cost of repav-ing the streets, avenues, or public places, in accord-ance with the provisions of this act, shall be included in the estimate of the department of public works, shall be appropriated by the board of estimate and apportionment, certified by the comptroller according to law, and inserted and included in the annual tax levies, and raised and collected by tax upon the estates subject to taxation in the city and county of New York, provided that the amount so appropriated and raised shall not exceed the sum of five hundred thousand dollars in any one single year.*

* See Appendix, G.

SEC 116. The annual salaries to be paid to persons herein named shall be as follows, and such salaries shall be in full for all services rendered by them to the city or county, in any capacity whatever:

To the mayor, twelve thousand dollars.

To the comptroller, ten thousand dollars.

To the commissioner of public works, ten thousand dollars.

To the corporation counsel, fifteen thousand dollars; and all legal costs collected by him shall be paid into the treasury of the city.

To the president of the board of police, eight thousand dollars.

To the commissioners of police, other than the president, six thousand dollars each.

To the president of the department of parks, six thousand five hundred dollars.

To the commissioners of parks, other than the president, nothing.

To the president of the fire department, seven thousand five hundred dollars.

To the fire commissioners, other than the president, five thousand dollars each.

To the president of the department of charities and correction, six thousand five hundred dollars.

To the commissioners of charities and correction, other than the president, five thousand dollars each.

To the president of the health department, six thousand five hundred dollars.

To the commissioner of health, other than the president, five thousand dollars.

[*Amended by sec. 23, chap.* 757, *laws of* 1873.] To the members of the board of aldermen, other than the president, four thousand dollars each, and to the members of the board of assistant aldermen, four thousand dollars each during their present term of office.

To the president of the board of aldermen, five thousand dollars.

To the president of the department of taxes and assessments, six thousand five hundred dollars.

To the commissioners of taxes and assessments, other than the president, five thousand dollars each.

To the president of the department of docks, six thousand five hundred dollars.

To the commissioners of docks, other than the president, three thousand dollars each.

[*Amended by sec.* 10, *chap.* 547, *laws of* 1874.] To the superintendent of buildings, six thousand five hundred dollars.

[*Amended by sec.* 23, *chap.* 757, *laws of* 1873.] To the commissioners of accounts, appointed by the mayor, three thousand dollars each.

7

Salary of
subordi-
nates.

Salary of
justices.

No subordinate in any department shall receive a greater salary than the highest salary paid to the head of the department, except the superintendent of police, whose salary shall not exceed ten thousand dollars per annum. The salaries of the justices of the district courts is hereby fixed at eight thousand dollars each per annum.

Expiration
of terms of
office.

SEC. 117. The terms of office of the present commissioners of police, except as hereinbefore expressly provided, fire commissioners, commissioners of charities and correction, commissioners of docks, commissioners of health, commissioners of parks, except as hereinbefore expressly provided, commissioners of taxes and assessments, superintendent of buildings, commissioner of jurors, city marshals, inspectors of weights and measures, members of all commissions or boards appointed to superintend the construction or repair of any public building in the city of New York, and of all commissions and boards heretofore appointed by the mayor, or the mayor and aldermen, save and except as hereinbefore expressly provided, and all members of any board, and all persons whatever heretofore appointed by the comptroller; of the chamberlain and all other officers hereinbefore authorized to be appointed by the mayor and board of aldermen, shall cease, terminate and expire on the first day of May, one thousand eight hundred and seventy-three, unless an appointment of a successor shall be sooner made as hereinbefore provided, in which case the term of office of the present incumbent shall cease, and the person so appointed shall enter upon his office on the first Monday succeeding such appointment; and no appointment of any subordinate in any department, made after the passage of this act and before said date, shall be valid beyond such date. The terms of office of the superintendent of police, the surgeons of police, the chief engineer of the fire department, the inspector of the fire apparatus, the superintendent of horses, and the superintendent of the repair yard in the fire department, the fire marshal and his deputies, shall cease and determine five days after the appointment of the head of the police and fire department respectively, and the terms of all subordinates in every department, except officers and men of the police force and the firemen and officers of the fire companies, shall cease and determine as soon as the heads of the department herein provided to be appointed shall appoint others in their places. Upon the appointment of their successors all the foregoing officers shall deliver over to such successors all property of every kind, and all books and papers in their use and possession, respectively, belonging to the city or any department thereof. The provisions of this section, relating to the vacating of any of the offices therein mentioned and the delivery of property, may be enforced by mandamus. But nothing in this section shall affect exceptions and savings in the twenty-fifth section of this act contained.

SEC. 118. The several departments shall continue to

possess the same powers and perform the same duties as heretofore, except as herein otherwise provided.

SEC. 119. The city of New York is hereby excepted from the provisions of an act entitled an act to establish a metropolitan police district, and to provide for the government thereof, passed April fifteen, eighteen hundred and fifty-seven, and of the acts amendatory thereof, and any sections of statutes and provisions of law which created said district are hereby repealed; and the city of New York is also hereby excepted from the provisions of the act entitled an act to create a metropolitan sanitary district and board of health therein, for the preservation of life and health, and to prevent spread of disease, passed February twenty-sixth, eighteen hundred and sixty-six, and of the acts amendatory thereof, and any sections of statutes and provisions of law which created said district are hereby repealed; and the city of New York is also hereby excepted from the provisions of an act entitled an act to create a metropolitan fire district, and establish a fire department therein, passed March thirtieth, eighteen hundred and sixty-five, and the acts amendatory thereof, and any sections of statutes and provisions of law

which created said district are hereby repealed. The act to amend the charter of the city of New York, passed April seventh, eighteen hundred and thirty; and the act to amend the charter of the city of New York, passed April second, eighteen hundred and forty-nine; and the act to amend an act entitled an act to amend the charter

of the city of New York, passed April second, eighteen
hundred and forty-nine, passed July eleventh, eighteen
hundred and fifty-one; and the act further to amend the
charter of the city of New York, passed April twelfth,
eighteen hundred and fifty-three; and the act supplementary to an act entitled an act further to amend the charter
of the city of New York, passed April twelfth, eighteen
hundred, and fifty-three, passed June fourteenth, eighteen
hundred and fifty-three; and the act to amend the charter
of the city of New York, passed April fourteen, eighteen
hundred and fifty-seven; and the act relative to the
charter of the city of New York, passed April three,
eighteen hundred and sixty-three; and the act to make
provision for the government of the city of New York,
passed June third, eighteen hundred and sixty-eight; and
the act entitled an act to reorganize the local government of the city of New York, passed April fifth,
eighteen hundred and seventy; and the act entitled an
act to make further provisions for the government of the
city of New York, passed April twenty-six, eighteen
hundred and seventy (save sections twenty-seven and
twenty-nine thereof); and the sixth section of an act
entitled an act concerning the police life insurance fund, Police life
insurance
and the powers and duties of the police department of fund.
the city of New York, passed March seventeen, eighteen
hundred and seventy-one; and the act entitled an act to
amend an act to reorganize the local government of the
city of New York, passed April fifth, eighteen hundred
and seventy, passed April the eighteenth, eighteen

Exception to repeal. hundred and seventy-one (save so much of section five thereof as relates to the establishment of a scale of water rents, and sections six and seven of said act); and the act entitled an act to make provision for the local governments of the city and county of New York, passed April nineteen, eighteen hundred and seventy-one, so far as said act relates to the city of New York, are hereby repealed; and all acts or parts of acts inconsistent with the provisions of this act are also hereby repealed; but the repeal of the act hereinabove cited of April fifth, eighteen hundred and seventy, and the acts passed subsequently thereto and hereinabove cited or referred to, so far as the same or either of them relate to any department by this act created, shall not take effect until the organization of any such

Dongan and Montgomerie charters. department as provided for in this act. The charters of the city of New York, known as Dongan and Montgomerie charters, so far as the same or either of them are now in force, not inconsistent with the provisions of this act, shall continue and remain in full force. This section shall not prejudice or affect any right accrued or legal proceeding commenced by reason of anything contained in the acts hereby repealed, and so accrued and commenced before this act takes effect, except so far as

Ordinances continued in force. herein specially provided for. The ordinances of the common council of the city of New York, in force on the first day of April, eighteen hundred and seventy, and all ordinances passed and adopted since the first day of May, eighteen hundred and seventy, and in force at the time of the passage of this act, are hereby revived and continued in full force as city ordinances, subject to modification, amendment or repeal by the common council of said city.*

SEC. 120. [*As amended by sec. 24, chap.* 757, *laws of* 1873.] This act shall take effect immediately, except as otherwise provided in the previous section; but nothing therein contained shall be in any wise held to extend or continue the term of office of any of the persons mentioned in section one hundred and seventeen, beyond the first day of May, eighteen hundred and seventy-three.

Terms of office mentioned in section 17 limited.

* See Appendix. O.

APPENDIX.

(A.)

Chapter 515.

AN ACT to amend an act entitled "An act to reorganize the local government of the city of New York," passed April thirtieth, eighteen hundred and seventy-three.

Passed May 21, 1874 ; three-fifths being present.

The People of the State of New York, represented in Senate and Assembly, do enact as follows :

SECTION 1. Section four of chapter three hundred and thirty five of the laws of eighteen hundred and seventy-three, entitled "An act to reorganize the local government of the city of New York," is hereby amended so as to read as follows:

§ 4. The board of aldermen now in office shall hold office until the first Monday in January, in the year eighteen hundred and seventy-five, the same being the term for which they were elected. There shall be twenty-two aldermen elected at the general state election which shall occur in the year eighteen hundred and seventy-four, three of whom shall be elected in each senate district, except the eighth senate district, and shall be residents of the district in which they are elected, but no voter shall vote for more than two of said aldermen. In the territory comprised within the eighth senate district, and the twenty-third and twenty-fourth wards, there shall be elected four aldermen, and the aldermen to be elected in said district may reside either in said eighth senate district or in the twenty-third and twenty-fourth wards, but no voter shall vote for more than three of the said

Aldermen.
term of
office.

When
elected.

aldermen. There shall also be elected six aldermen at large to be voted for on a separate ballot, but no voter shall vote for more than four of the said aldermen at large, and the voters of the twenty-third and twenty-fourth wards of said city are hereby authorized and empowered to vote for aldermen at large. The members of the board of aldermen shall hold office for the space of one year, and shall take office on the first Monday in January, next succeeding their election, at noon. Annually thereafter, at the general state election, there shall be elected a full board of aldermen as hereinbefore provided. Any

vacancy now existing, or which may hereafter occur, in *either* * the *board of aldermen* by reason of the death or resignation, or of any other cause, of a member of either of said boards, shall be filled by election by the board in which such vacancy exists or shall arise, by a vote of a majority of all the members elected to said board; and the person so elected to fill any such vacancy shall serve until the first day of January, at noon, next succeeding the first general election occurring not less than thirty days after the happening of such vacancy, but not beyond the expiration of the term in which the vacancy shall occur; and at such election a person shall be elected to serve the remainder, if any, of such unexpired term. From and after the termination of the term of office of the board of assistant aldermen as herein provided, the board of aldermen shall alone constitute the common council and shall exercise the entire legislative powers of the said city.

SEC. 4.* This act shall take effect immediately.

* So in the original.

(B.)

Chapter 304.

An Act to consolidate the government of the city and county of New York, and further to regulate the same.

Passed April 30, 1874 ; three-fifths being present.

The People of the State of New York, represented in Senate and Assembly, do enact as follows :

SECTION 1. The county of New York and the corporation known by the name of " the mayor, aldermen, and commonalty of the city of New York " shall be one body corporate and politic by the said name; and all the rights, property, interests, claims, and demands of the county of New York, and of the supervisors or board of supervisors of the said county of New York, are hereby vested in and shall henceforth belong to the said corporation ; but nothing contained in this act shall abrogate or impair or in anywise affect any existing right or interest, except to vest it in the said corporation. *Consolidation.* *Existing rights unimpaired.*

SEC. 2. For all purposes the local administration and government of the city and county of New York shall be in and be performed by the one corporation aforesaid. All charges and liabilities now existing against said county, or which may hereafter arise or accrue in said city and county of New York, and which, but for this act, would be charges against or liabilities of said county, shall be henceforth deemed and taken to be charges against or liabilities of said corporation, and shall be defrayed or answered unto by it. All bonds, stocks, contracts and obligations of the said county and of the said board of supervisors, now existing, shall henceforth be deemed such of and against said corporation, and all such that are or may be authorized or required to be hereafter issued or entered into, shall be issued or entered into by and in the name of the said corporation. *County charges and liabilities merged in the city corporation.*

SEC. 3. All the powers and duties that now are or hereafter may be conferred or charged upon the board of supervisors of the said city and county shall be exercised and performed by the board of aldermen of said city as such, subject, nevertheless, to the like power of approval or rejection by the mayor of said city, as is or may be required by law in respect to acts of the common council of said city, except that when by the constitution or laws of this state any action is specifically required to be taken by the board of supervisors of said city and county, which cannot, under any power conferred by this act or otherwise, be taken in any other manner, such action may be taken by the said board of aldermen as the board of supervisors of the said city and county.

Powers and duties of board of supervisors transferred to board of aldermen.

SEC. 4. All funds and moneys now held by or payable to any officer as county treasurer of the said city and county shall henceforth be deemed to be held by him solely as the funds and moneys of said corporation, except such funds and moneys as shall be held by and payable into the treasury of the state of New York.

Funds held by county treasurer.

SEC. 5. This act shall take effect immediately.

(C.)

Chapter 305.

AN ACT explanatory of " An act to consolidate the government of the city and county of New York, and further to regulate the same."

Passed April 30, 1874 ; three-fifths being present.

The People of the State of New York, represented in Senate and Assembly, do enact as follows:

SECTION 1. Nothing in the act entitled " An act to consolidate the government of the city and county of New York, and further to regulate the same," shall be construed to affect the election and appointment of county officers whose election or appointment is provided for County officers. by the constitution of this state, the apportionment of members of assembly, or any other purposes for which the city and county of New York is recognized in the constitution as one of the counties of this state.

SEC. 2. This act shall take effect immediately.

———

(D.)

Chapter 757.

AN ACT to amend chapter three hundred and thirty-five of the laws of eighteen hundred and seventy-three, entitled "An act to reorganize the local government of the city of New York," passed April thirteenth,* eighteen hundred and seventy-three.

Passed June 13, 1873 ; three-fifths being present.

The People of the State of New York, represented in Senate and Assembly, do enact as follows :

SECTION 1. Section four of chapter three hundred and thirty-five of the laws of eighteen hundred and seventy-three, entitled "An act to reorganize the local government of the city of New York," passed April thirtieth, eighteen hundred and seventy-three, is hereby amended (see chap. 515, Laws 1874).

SEC. 2. Section seven of said chapter is hereby amended so as to read as follows :

§ 7. Every member expelled from either board shall thereby forfeit Expulsion. all his rights and powers as alderman or assistant alderman.

* So in original.

SEC. 3. Section eight of said chapter is hereby amended so as to read as follows :

Meetings.

§ 8. The stated and occasional meetings of each board shall be regulated by its own resolutions and rules, and both boards may meet at the same time or on different days, as they may severally deem expedient.

SEC. 4. Section ten of said chapter is hereby amended so as to read as follows :

§ 10. The mayor shall return such ordinance or resolution to the board in which it originated within ten days after receiving it, or at the next meeting of such board after the expiration of said ten days.

Clerk of board of aldermen, his duties.

SEC. 5. The first period or sentence of section fifteen is hereby amended so as to read as follows : " The clerk of the board of aldermen shall, by virtue of his office, be clerk of the common council and of the board of supervisors, and shall perform all the duties heretofore performed by the clerk of the common council, except such as shall be assigned to the clerk of the board of assistant aldermen, without additional compensation to that paid him as clerk of the board of aldermen."

SEC. 6. The tenth subdivision of the seventeenth section of said chapter is hereby amended, by adding thereto, at the end thereof, the words following : " and to provide for regulating, grading, flagging, curbing, guttering and lighting streets, roads, places and avenues."

SEC. 7. Section twenty is hereby amended so as to read as follows :

Mayor to continue in office.

§ 20. The mayor in office on April twenty-ninth, eighteen hundred and seventy-three, shall hold office until the first day of January, in the year eighteen hundred and seventy-five. The mayor shall be the chief executive officer of the corporation ; shall be elected at a general election, and hold his office for the term of two years, commencing on the first day of January next after his election. The first election for mayor under this act shall be at the general election in November, in the year eighteen hundred and seventy-four.

SEC. 8. The twenty-ninth section of the said chapter is hereby amended by adding at the end of the seventh clause or sentence of said section the words: "But this provision shall not apply to work done or supplies furnished, not involving the expenditure of more than one thousand dollars, pursuant to section ninety-one of this act." And the said section is further amended by adding at the end thereof the words following: "The comptroller shall furnish to each head of department, weekly, a statement of the unexpended balance of the appropriation of his department; wages and salaries, including payments for the board of education, may be paid upon pay-rolls, upon which each person named thereon shall separately receipt for the amount paid to such person, and in every case of payment upon a pay-roll, the warrant for the aggregate amount of wages and salaries included therein may be made payable to the superintendent, principal teacher, foreman or other officer designated for the purpose."

Comptroller to furnish weekly statement.

Wages and salaries may be paid upon pay-rolls.

SEC. 9. Section seventy-three of the said chapter is hereby amended by striking out of the same the words "ninety-seven" and inserting in place thereof the words "ninety-one."

SEC. 10. Section seventy-five of said chapter is hereby amended so as to read as follows:

§ 75. No money belonging to the city, or city and county, of New York, raised by taxation upon the property of the citizens thereof, shall be appropriated in aid of any religious or denominational school, neither shall any property, real or personal, belonging to said city, or said city and county, be disposed of to any such school, except upon the sale thereof at public auction after the same has been duly advertised, at which sale such school shall be the highest bidder, and upon payment of the sum so bid into the city treasury; neither shall any property belonging to the city, or city and county, be leased to any school under the control of any religious or denominational institution, except upon such terms as city property may be leased to private parties after the same has been duly advertised.

Money not to be appropriated to religious or denominational schools.

SEC. 11. Section seventy-eight of said chapter is hereby amended so as to read as follows :

Fire department, qualifications for membership.

§ 78. No person shall ever be appointed to membership in the fire department, or continue to hold membership therein, who is not a citizen of the United States, or who has ever been convicted of crime, or who cannot read and write understandingly in the English language, or who shall not have resided within the state one year.

SEC. 12. Section eighty-second of said chapter is hereby amended by adding thereto as follows : "The authority, duty, and powers conferred or enjoined upon the metropolitan board of health by chapter seventy-four of the laws of eighteen hundred and sixty-six, and the several acts amendatory thereof, and by any other subsequent laws of this state, and upon the several officers and members of said board, not inconsistent with the provisions of this act, are hereby conferred upon and vested in or enjoined upon, and shall hereafter be exclusively exercised in the city of New York, by the health department and board of health, created by this act, and by the officers of the said board of health and the said health department, and the same are to be exercised in the manner specified in the said chapter seventy-four of the laws of eighteen hundred and sixty-six, and the several acts amendatory thereof, and by any other subsequent laws of the state, and in conformity to the provisions of this act."

Board of health, powers.

SEC. 13. The eighty-third section of said chapter is hereby amended by striking out therefrom the words "for the construction."

SEC. 14. The eighty-fourth section of said chapter is hereby amended by striking out therefrom the word "four."

SEC. 15. The eighty-fifth section of said chapter is hereby amended so as to read as follows :

§ 85. There shall be a department called the "department of buildings," which shall be under the control of an officer who shall be known as the "superintendent of buildings," and shall be the same person nominated as "commissioner of buildings" by the mayor of the city of

Superintendent of buildings.

New York, on the fifteenth day of May, one thousand eight hundred and seventy-three, and confirmed by the board of aldermen of said city, on the sixteenth day of May, one thousand eight hundred and seventy-three; which said superintendent shall hold office for the full term for which said commissioner was appointed, unless sooner removed, as provided by law, for the removal of heads of departments.

The eighty-sixth section of said chapter is hereby amended so as to read as follows:

§ 86. Each and all the powers and duties of said department, and all its officers and employees and subordinates, and their qualifications, shall continue and be exercised as non-authorized by special laws in relation to buildings in the city of New York, and it shall not be lawful for any officer or employee in said department to be engaged in conducting or carrying on business as an architect, carpenter, mason or builder while holding office in said department. The one hundred and sixteenth section of said chapter is hereby amended by striking out therefrom the words "to the commissioner" and "surveyor" of buildings four thousand dollars "each," and inserting in lieu thereof "to the superintendent of buildings four thousand dollars." *Department of buildings, powers and duties.* *Fees.*

Sec. 16. Section ninety-six of said chapter is hereby amended by inserting after the word "government," in the first line thereof, the following words, viz., "except the city marshals." Said section is hereby further amended by adding at the end thereof the following: "But nothing herein contained shall be construed so as to repeal, modify or otherwise affect the provisions of the fourteenth section of chapter seven hundred and forty-two of the laws of eighteen hundred and seventy-one."

Sec. 17. Section one hundred and two is hereby amended by inserting in the third section thereof, after the words, but if said property be "market property," the following words, viz., "excepting the market between Sixteenth and Seventeenth streets, east of Avenue C, the market in Gouverneur slip, and the market in Old slip." *Sale or lease of market property.*

8

SEC. 18. Section one hundred and three of said chapter is hereby repealed.

SEC. 19. Section one hundred and eleven of the said chapter is hereby amended by adding at the end thereof the following: "Nothing herein contained shall apply to any printing or supplies of stationery for any department where, by the concurrent vote of the mayor, commissioner of public works, and corporation counsel, it shall be decided to have such printing done or such stationery furnished without contract; but in such cases such printing and stationery shall be procured in such manner and on such terms and conditions as the said officers shall deem to be for the best interests of the city."

Printing and stationery.

SEC. 20. Section one hundred and twelve of said chapter is hereby amended by inserting in the first sentence of the same, after the words "and branch thereof," the following words, viz., "and the board of education;" and also by inserting in the fourth sentence, after the words "the heads of departments," the following words, viz., "and the board of education." The said section is hereby further amended by adding at the end thereof the following: "Any balances of appropriations remaining unexpended, after allowing sufficient to satisfy all claims payable therefrom, may, at any time, after the expiration of the year for which they were made, be transferred by the comptroller, with the approval of said board of estimate and apportionment, to the general fund of the city, and applied to the reduction of taxation."

Unexpended balances of appropriation.

SEC. 21. Section one hundred and fourteen of said chapter shall not be construed to apply to civil or consulting engineers who may be appointed to superintend any specific work on the part of the city of New York.

SEC. 22. Section one hundred and fifteen of said chapter is hereby amended so as to read as follows:

Repaving streets, etc., at expense of owners, to be done only on petition.

§ 115. No street, avenue, or public place in the city of New York, which has been once paved, and the expense thereof paid for by the owners of the adjoining property, by assessment, shall hereafter be paved at their expense, nor shall any assessment therefor be imposed, unless the same shall be petitioned for by a majority of the owners of the property (who shall also be the owners of a majority of the front feet) on the line of the proposed improvement; and any ordinance or resolution heretofore passed for any repavement, which has not been petitioned for by a majority of the owners of the adjoining property to be affected, and for which no contract has been entered into or award of contract made, is hereby declared to be inoperative and void. Except for repairs, no patented pavement shall be laid, and no patented article shall be advertised for, contracted for, or purchased, except under such circumstances that there can be a fair and reasonable opportunity for competition, the conditions to secure which shall be prescribed by the board of estimate and apportionment.

SEC. 23. That portion of section one hundred and sixteen of said chapter referring to the salary of members of the board of aldermen and members of the board of assistant aldermen, and that portion of said section referring to the salary of the president of board of aldermen, are hereby amended so as to read as follows:

To the members of the board of aldermen, other than the president, *Salaries.* four thousand dollars each; and to the members of the board of assistant aldermen, four thousand dollars each, during their present term of office.

To the president of the board of aldermen, five thousand dollars.

That portion of said section referring to the salary of the commis- *Salaries of* sioner of accounts is hereby amended so as to read as follows: *commissioners of accounts.*

To the commissioners of accounts appointed by the mayor, three thousand dollars each.

The last subdivision of said section one hundred and sixteen is hereby amended so as to read as follows:

No subordinate in any department shall receive a greater salary than the highest salary paid to the head of the department, except the superintendent of the police, whose salary shall not exceed ten thousand dollars per annum.

Salary of justices.

The salary of the justices of the district courts is hereby fixed at eight thousand dollars each per annum.

SEC. 24. Section one hundred and twenty of said chapter is hereby amended by striking out therefrom the words "in section one hundred and twenty-two," and inserting in place thereof the words "in section one hundred and seventeen."

SEC. 25. This act shall take effect immediately.

(E.)

Chapter 129.

AN ACT to amend an act entitled "An act to reorganize the local government of the city of New York," passed April thirtieth, eighteen hundred and seventy-three.

Passed April 21, 1875; three-fifths being present.

The People of the State of New York, represented in Senate and Assembly, do enact as follows:

SECTION 1. Section thirty-five of chapter three hundred and thirty-five of the laws of eighteen hundred and seventy-three, entitled "An act to reorganize the local government of the city of New York," passed April thirtieth, eighteen hundred and seventy-three, is hereby amended so as to read as follows:

City chamberlain, duties of.

§ 35. The said chamberlain and mayor and the comptroller of the city of New York, shall, by a majority vote, by written notice, to the comptroller, designate the banks or trust companies in which all moneys of the mayor, aldermen, and commonalty of the said city and county of New York shall be deposited, and may, by like notice, in writing, from time to time, change the banks or trust companies thus designated; but no such bank or trust company shall be designated

unless its officers shall agree to pay into the city treasury interest on
the daily balances at a rate to be fixed by the mayor and chamberlain,
and the said comptroller of the city of New York, by a majority vote,
which rate shall not be less than two and one-half per cent. The said
chamberlain shall keep books showing the receipts of moneys from all
sources, and designating the sources of the same, and also showing the
amounts paid from time to time on account of the several appropriations; and no warrant shall be paid on account of any appropriation
after the amount authorized to be raised for that specific purpose shall
have been expended. The said chamberlain shall once in each week
report in writing to the mayor and to the comptroller all moneys
received by him, the amounts of all warrants paid by him since his last
report, and the amount remaining to the credit of the city and county
of New York respectively. The said chamberlain shall receive the sum
of thirty thousand dollars annually, and no more, for all his services as Salary.
chamberlain of said city and as county treasurer of the county of New
York in lieu of salary and of all interest, fees, commissions and emoluments; and all such interest, fees, commissions and emoluments shall
be accounted for and paid over by him to the city treasury. He may
appoint and remove at pleasure, a deputy chamberlain and such clerks May appoint.
and assistants as may be necessary, whose salaries, together with all clerks.
the expenses of his office, shall be paid wholly by him, and shall in no
case be a public charge. The commissions provided by law, and
received by him for receiving and paying over the state taxes, and all
interest accrued on deposits shall be paid by him to the commissioners
of the sinking fund.

SEC. 2. This act shall take effect immediately.

(F.)

Chapter 300.

An Act to amend chapter three hundred and thirty-five of the laws of eighteen hundred and seventy-three, entitled "An act to reorganize the local government of the city of New York," passed April thirtieth, eighteen hundred and seventy-three, and the acts amendatory thereof.

Passed April 30, 1874 : three-fifths being present.

The People of the State of New York, represented in Senate and Assembly, do enact as follows :

Section 1. Section thirty-nine of chapter three hundred and thirty-five of the laws of eighteen hundred and seventy-three, entitled "An act to reorganize the local government of the city of New York," passed April thirtieth, eighteen hundred and seventy-three, is hereby amended so as to read as follows :

Appointment of police commissioners.

§ 39. The police department shall have for its head a board to consist of four persons, to be known as police commissioners of the city of New York, who shall, except those first appointed, hold their offices for six years, unless sooner removed as herein provided. The office of the police commissioner of the city of New York, whose term of office expires on the first day of May, eighteen hundred and seventy-four, is hereby abolished on and after said date; the police department, on and after the first day of May, eighteen hundred and seventy-four, shall be under the charge and control of four commissioners, who shall perform all the duties and exercise all the powers now by law conferred or imposed upon the police deparment of the city of New York.

Sec. 2. Section eighty-four of chapter three hundred and thirty-five of the laws of eighteen hundred and seventy-three, entitled "An act to reorganize the local government of the city of New York," passed April thirtieth, eighteen hundred and seventy-three, is hereby amended so as to read as follows:

§ 84. This department shall be under the charge of a board, to consist of four members, who, except those first appointed, shall hold their offices for five years, unless sooner removed as herein provided. The office of the commissioner of parks, whose term of office expires on the first day of May, eighteen hundred and seventy-four, is hereby abolished on and after said date. The department of public parks on and after the first day of May, eighteen hundred and seventy-four, shall be under the charge and control of four commissioners, who shall perform all the duties and exercise all ths powers now by law conferred or imposed upon the department of public parks of the city of New York. *Park commissioners. Office of commissioner of parks abolished.*

SEC. 3. The mayor of said city shall hereafter appoint, without confirmation of the board of aldermen, a person or persons to fill any vacancy or vacancies which now exists or may hereafter occur from death, resignation or cause other than the expiration of the full term in any office to which, of the provisions of the twenty-fifth section of chapter three hundred and thirty-five of the laws of eighteen hundred and seventy-three, he is empowered to appoint by and with the consent of the board of aldermen. *Vacancies, how filled.*

SEC. 4 This act shall take effect immediately.

(G.)

Chapter 476.

An Act to provide for a uniform system for the repavement of streets, avenues, and public places in the city of New York.

Passed May 28, 1875 ; three fifths being present.

The People of the State of New York, represented in Senate and Assembly, do enact as follows :

Powers of board of aldermen to direct repavement of streets and avenues.

SECTION 1. Whenever the commissioner of public works of the city of New York shall certify and report to the board of aldermen of said city that the safety, health, or convenience of the public requires the repavement of any streets, avenues, or public places in said city, said board of aldermen shall have the power to direct by ordinance or resolution the repavement of said streets, avenues, or public places, in the

Materials.

manner specified and of the materials approved of and recommended by said commissioner of public works, which work shall be done by and

Work done under direction of department of public works.

under the direction of the department of public works, according to law. In case any of the streets, avenues, or public places in said city shall have been once paved, and the expense thereof assessed upon the owners of adjoining and benefited property, the cost of the repaving thereof shall be borne by a general assessment upon all taxable property

The cost of repaving raised and collected by tax.

in said city. The cost of repaving the streets, avenues, or public places, in accordance with the provisions of this act, shall be included in the estimate of the department of public works, shall be appropriated by the board of estimate and apportionment, certified by the comptroller according to law, and inserted and included in the annual tax levies, and raised and collected by tax upon the estates subject to taxation in the city and county of New York, provided that the amount so appropriated and raised shall not exceed the sum of five hundred thousand dollars in any one single year.

Sec. 2. All acts and parts of acts which are inconsistent with the provisions of this act are hereby repealed so far as they relate to this act.

Sec. 3. This act shall take effect immediately.

———

(II.)

Chapter 726.

An Act to provide for the more effectual extinguishment of fires in the city of New York.

Passed June 12, 1873 ; three-fifths being present.

The People of the State of New York, represented in Senate and Assembly, do enact as follows :

SECTION 1. The fire commissioners of the city of New York are hereby empowered and directed to organize, in the fire department of the city of New York, a corps to be known as the corps of sappers and miners. Said corps shall be composed of not exceeding three members, either officers or private firemen, of each company in said fire department, and said members shall be appointed by said fire commissioners, upon the nomination of the chief engineer of said fire department. *Fire department to organize corps of sappers and miners.*

SEC. 2. The said fire commissioners shall appoint a suitable officer, who shall be skilled in the use of explosives, whose duty it shall be to instruct and drill said corps in the use of explosives, and to give said corps such other instruction as may be required to qualify them to effectually discharge the duties imposed upon them by this act. Such officer shall receive an annual salary of two thousand dollars, and such salary shall be raised and paid in the same manner as the salaries of the other officers appointed by the said fire commissioners. *Drill officer to be appointed. Salary.*

SEC. 3. Whenever, under and by virtue of the acts relating to the extinguishment of fires in the said city of New York, the destruction or pulling down of any building or buildings shall be deemed necessary, and shall be ordered by the engineer in command at any fire in said

Duties of sappers and miners.

city, it shall be the duty of said corps, or any member or members thereof, by the direction of the said engineer in command at such fire, to level and destroy such building or buildings by the use of explosives, for the purpose of arresting the spread of such fire, and it shall be lawful for them to enter and take possession of the same for such purposes.

Depots for storage of explosives.

SEC. 4. The said fire commissioners shall establish in the city of New York one or more depots for the storage and safe keeping of such explosives as may be required for the use of said corps, and may limit the quantity of any such explosives to be kept at any one of such depots.

SEC. 5. All acts or portions of acts inconsistent with the provisions of this act are hereby repealed.

SEC. 6. This act shall take effect immediately.

———

(I.)

Chapter 839.

AN ACT to authorize the board of health of the health department of the city of New York to make a contract to remove the contents of sinks and privies in said city.

Passed June 26, 1873 ; three-fifths being present.

The People of the State of New York, represented in Senate and Assembly, do enact as follows :

Board of health authorized to contract for removing contents of sinks and privies.

SECTION 1. The board of health of the health department of the city of New York is hereby authorized to contract with any responsible person or persons, up to the first of May, eighteen hundred and seventy-five (or the sooner determination of a contract made by and between the mayor, aldermen, and commonalty of said city of the one part, and Daniel Gallagher of the other part, bearing date May first, eighteen hundred and sixty-five, by which the former agreed, among other things. to deliver to the latter all the contents of sinks and privies, as therein specified, until the first of May, eighteen hundred and seventy-five), to furnish during the day, as well as the night, the necessary boats for receiving and removing, and to remove and deliver all the contents of sinks and privies, as Thomas Andrews, by a contract, between him and the mayor, aldermen, and commonalty of said city, bearing date May first. eighteen hundred and sixty-five, agreed to furnish for receiving and removing, and to remove and deliver such contents, and in relation thereto, at a price not exceeding thirty-three thousand dollars per annum, to be paid in equal monthly installments, and to require and receive satisfactory security in such form and amount as such board may approve for the faithful performance, by the person or persons to whom such contract may be awarded, of all and every of the provisions of such contract on his or their part. For any breach of said contract by such contracting party or parties, an action *Penalty for breach of contract.* may be prosecuted in the name of the mayor, alderman,* and commonalty of the city of New York, in any court having jurisdiction thereof, against said party or parties, his or their sureties, or both, to recover the damages sustained by such breach or breaches, as the same may from time to time occur; but nothing in this section contained shall be construed to legalize the contract or contracts for the purposes herein stated.

SEC. 2. This act shall take effect immediately.

* So in original.

(**J**.)

Chapter 759.

As Act to provide for the completion of county buildings in the city and county of New York.

Passed June 13, 1873 ; three-fifths being present.

The People of the State of New York, represented in Senate and Assembly, do enact as follows :

Commissioners of buildings.

SECTION 1. The terms of office of each and every commissioner heretofore appointed for the erection of buildings for county purposes in the city and county of New York shall be and are hereby declared to be terminated. And the persons nominated by the mayor of the city of New York, and by and with the consent of the board of aldermen

How appointed.

appointed as such commissioners, pursuant to chapter three hundred and thirty-five of the laws of eighteen hundred and seventy-three, shall be commissioners for the purposes for which they are appointed,

Powers and duties.

and shall have and perform all the powers and duties given to such commissioners by the existing provisions of law. The compensation of

Compensation.

such commissioners shall be fixed by the board of estimate and apportionment, but shall in no case exceed the sum of two thousand dollars each per annum.

SEC. 2. This act shall take effect immediately.

(K.)

Chapter 631.

AN ACT to amend chapter seven hundred and fifty-seven of the laws of eighteen hundred and seventy-three, entitled "An act to amend chapter three hundred and thirty-five of the laws of eighteen hundred and seventy-three, entitled 'An act to reorganize the local government of the city of New York,'" passed April thirteenth, eighteen hundred and seventy-three.

Passed June 21, 1875 ; three-fifths being present.

The People of the State of New York, represented in Senate and Assembly, do enact as follows :

SECTION 1. Section nineteen of chapter seven hundred and fifty-seven of the laws of eighteen hundred and seventy-three, entitled " An act to amend chapter three hundred and thirty-five of the laws of eighteen hundred and seventy-three, entitled ' An act to reorganize the local government of the city of New York,'" passed April thirteenth, eighteen hundred and seventy-three, is hereby amended so as to read as follows :

§ 19. Section one hundred and eleven of the said chapter is hereby amended by adding at the end thereof the following : " Nothing herein contained shall apply to any printing or supplies of stationery for the mayor, aldermen, and commonalty of the city of New York, where, by the concurrent vote of the mayor, counsel to the corporation, and the commissioner of public works, it shall be decided to have such printing done or such stationery furnished without contract let after advertisements for bids or proposals ; but in such cases such printing shall be done and such stationery procured in the manner, and on such terms and conditions as the said officers shall deem to be for the best interests of the city."

Printing, etc., otherwise than by contract.

SEC. 2. This act shall take effect immediately.

(**L.**)

Chapter 758.

An Act in relation to the city of New York.

Passed June 13, 1873; three-fifths being present.

The People of the State of New York, represented in Senate and Assembly, do enact as follows :

Powers of board of estimate and apportionment. SECTION 1. The board of estimate and apportionment constituted by section one hundred and twelve of chapter three hundred and thirty-five of the laws of eighteen hundred and seventy-three, is hereby authorized at any time before the first day of July next, by the concurrent vote of all the members of said board, to reconsider, revise and redetermine any estimate made under the provisions of section eight of chapter five hundred and seventy-four of the laws of eighteen hundred and seventy-one, and the estimates so reconsidered, revised and redetermined and approved by the concurrent vote of all the members of said board, shall thereby become appropriated as the amount of money required to defray all the various expenses necessary for conducting the various boards, commissions and departments, whether executive. judicial, legislative or administrative, of the city government, and also for paying the interest on the city debt, and the principal of such debt falling due, and for providing for charitable or other objects, and said amount shall be established and be the amount to be raised for such purposes by tax within the city and county of New York for the year eighteen hundred and seventy-three, and the amount thus established shall be certified to the board of supervisors by the comptroller, and the said board of supervisors are hereby empowered **Supervisors to raise amount appropriated by taxation.** and directed to cause the amount so certified to be raised and collected in the year eighteen hundred and seventy-three by tax upon estates, real and personal, within the city and county of New York subject to taxation.

SEC. 2. Nothing contained in any act heretofore passed shall prevent the payment of arrears of rent for armories and drill-rooms in cases in which the board of supervisors, since the first day of January, eighteen hundred and seventy-two, shall have authorized the leases of such armories and drill-rooms to be canceled and the public use thereof to cease, on condition of the payment of such arrears of rents, or in cases in which the premises shall have been continuously occupied as armories or drill-rooms until the present time, or until the expiration of the terms for which the same were leased. *Arrears of rent for armories and drill-rooms.*

SEC. 3. Nothing contained in section one hundred and eleven of chapter three hundred and thirty-five of the laws of eighteen hundred and seventy-three, shall prevent the publication of any advertisement required by law; provided, however, that no such publication shall be made unless the same is authorized by a concurrent vote of the mayor, corporation counsel and commissioner of public works. *Advertising.*

SEC. 4. This act shall take effect immediately.

———

(M.)

Chapter 308.

AN ACT in relation to the estimates and apportionments for the support of the government of the city of New York.

Passed May 1, 1874; three-fifths being present.

The People of the State of New York, represented in Senate and Assembly, do enact as follows:

SECTION 1. The board of estimate and apportionment constituted by section one hundred and twelve of chapter three hundred and thirty-five of the laws of eighteen hundred and seventy-three, is hereby authorized, at any time before the first day of July, eighteen hundred and seventy four, by the concurrent vote of all the members of said

Estimate for 1874 to be revised and corrected.

board, to reconsider, revise, and redetermine the estimate for the year eighteen hundred and seventy-four, heretofore made under the provisions of said act, and of section twenty of chapter seven hundred and fifty-seven of the laws of eighteen hundred and seventy-three, and the amount of the estimate so reconsidered, revised, and redetermined and approved by the concurrent vote of all the members of said board, shall thereby become appropriated as the amount of money required to defray the expenses of conducting the public business of the city of New York and of the various departments, boards, and commissions thereof, whether administrative, executive, or judicial, and for paying the interest on the city debt and the principal of such debt falling due in and for the year eighteen hundred and seventy-four, and for all liabilities of the city of New York, by reason of the annexation

Taxes, how appropriated.

thereto of territory lately a part of Westchester county, and for the expenses of conducting the public business of said annexed territory for and during said year, and the liabilities incurred by the board of education of said territory during the year eighteen hundred and seventy-three, which are hereby made an obligation of the city of New York ; and the aggregate amount of said estimate, after deducting the estimated amount of the revenues of the general fund of the city of New York, not otherwise specifically appropriated by law, including surplus revenues of the sinking fund for the payment of interest on the city debt, shall be established and be the amount to be raised for all such purposes, by tax, within the city and county of New York for the year eighteen hundred and seventy-four, and the amount thus established shall be certified to the board of supervisors by the comp-

Apportionments, when certified, to be raised by tax.

troller ; and the said board of supervisors are hereby empowered and directed to cause the amount so certified to be raised and collected in the year eighteen hundred and seventy-four, by tax upon the estates by law subject to taxation within the city and county of New York. But the aggregate amount of the estimates for the year eighteen hundred and seventy-four, to be made by the said board of estimate and apportionment, shall not exceed the amount of the estimate heretofore made by the said board, as aforesaid. In the estimate, so to be made, no sum shall be included, except the same be appropriated for a specified department or purpose, and no sum shall be appropriated for special contingencies.

Special contingencies.

Sec. 2. The said board of estimate and apportionment shall have the power at any time to transfer any appropriation for any year which may be found, by the head of the department for which such appropriation shall have been made, to be in excess of the amount required or deemed to be necessary for the purposes or objects thereof, to such other purposes or objects for which the appropriations are insufficient, or such as may require the same ; and if it is found at the time when the estimate is made of the expenses of conducting the public business of the city of New York for the next succeeding fiscal year, that there will be a surplus or balance remaining unexpended of any appropriation then existing at the end of the current fiscal year, such surplus may be applied to like purposes in the next succeeding year.

Unexpended appropriations may be transferred.

Sec. 3. The amount of money required by provision of section eight of chapter seven hundred and two of the laws of eighteen hundred and seventy-two, to be included in the amount to be raised by tax in the year eighteen hundred and seventy-three, by section four of chapter ninety-five, laws of eighteen hundred and seventy-three, to be included in the amount to be raised by tax in the year eighteen hundred and seventy-four, shall, instead of being raised in eighteen hundred and seventy-four, be raised and included in the amount to be levied by tax in the year eighteen hundred and seventy-five ; and in anticipation of the levy and collection thereof, the comptroller is authorized and required to issue revenue bonds for such amounts as may from time to time be required to be paid pursuant to the provisions of section seven of said chapter seven hundred and two of the laws of eighteen hundred and seventy-two, such revenue bonds to be paid from the amounts so to be raised by tax in the year eighteen hundred and seventy-five. This act shall not be construed to authorize said board to reduce or transfer any appropriation heretofore or hereafter made for the purposes of carrying out the provisions of the acts mentioned in this section ; and

Comptroller to issue revenue bonds in lieu of taxes for 1874.

9

except as herein modified, all the provisions of chapter seven hundred and two of the laws of eighteen hundred and seventy-two are confirmed and continued in full force and effect.

Tax levy for 1874 limited.

SEC. 4. No moneys shall be levied and raised in the year eighteen hundred and seventy-four by tax within the county of New York for the purposes authorized by section seventeen of chapter five hundred and thirty-five of the laws of eighteen hundred and seventy-three, excepting such expenses as may have been actually incurred by the commission in said act named.

SEC. 5. This act shall take effect immediately.

(N.)

Chapter 303.

AN ACT in relation to the estimates and apportionment for the support of the government of the county of New York.

Passed April 30, 1874; three-fifths being present.

The People of the State of New York, represented in Senate and Assembly, do enact as follows:

Estimate and appropriations, how levied and collected.

SECTION 1. The board of estimate and apportionment constituted by section one of chapter seven hundred and seventy-nine of the laws of eighteen hundred and seventy-three, is hereby authorized by a concurrent vote of all the members thereof, at any time before the first day of July, eighteen hundred and seventy-four, to reconsider, revise, and redetermine the estimate heretofore made under the provisions of said act for the year eighteen hundred and seventy-four, and the estimates so reconsidered, revised, and redetermined and approved by the concurrent vote of all said members, shall thereby be appropriated as the amount of money required to defray all the various expenses necessary for conducting the county government, and for supporting inmates of asylums, reformatories, and charitable institutions chargeable by existing provisions of law upon the county of New York, and for defraying all legal charges against the county of New York under special laws, and also for paying the interest on the county debt and the principal of such debt falling due in the year eighteen hundred and seventy-four, and the proportion of the state tax for the year eighteen hundred and seventy-four payable by said county, and thereupon to fix and determine the amount of such estimates and various expenses and charges after deducting the estimated amount of county revenue not otherwise appropriated by law, which amount, when so fixed and determined, shall be certified to the board of supervisors of the county of New York by the Comptroller; and said board of supervisors are hereby empowered and directed to cause the amount so certified, to be levied and collected in the year eighteen hundred and seventy-four, by tax upon the estates within the county of New York subject to taxation. But the aggregate amount of the estimate for the year eighteen hundred and seventy- four, to be made by the said board of estimate and apportionment, shall not exceed the amount of the estimate heretofore made by the said board as aforesaid. In the estimate so to be made no sum shall be included, except the same be appropriated for a specified department or purpose, and no sum shall be appropriated for special contingencies.

Estimates for 1874 limited.

SEC. 2. The said board of estimate and apportionment shall have the power at any time to transfer any appropriation for any year which may be found by the head of the department for which such appropriation shall have been made to be in excess of the amount required or deemed to be necessary for the purposes or objects thereof, to such other purposes or objects for which the appropriations are insufficient, or such as may require the same; and if it is found at the time when the estimate is made of the expenses of conducting the public business of the county of New York for the next succeeding fiscal year, that there will be a surplus or balance remaining unexpended of any appropriation then existing at the end of the current fiscal year, such surplus may be applied to like purposes in the next succeeding year.

Appropriations may be transferred.

SEC. 3. The payment of the bonds authorized by section three of chapter ninety-five of the laws of eighteen hundred and seventy-three, instead of commencing in the year eighteen hundred and seventy-four, as therein provided, shall have the first installment thereof paid in the year eighteen hundred and seventy-six, and the other installments annually thereafter.

Change of time for paying installment on bonds.

SEC. 4. This act shall take effect immediately.

(O.)

Chapter 326.

AN ACT to limit in certain respects the effect of certain repealing clauses in a bill which has passed the Senate and Assembly, at the present session, entitled "An act to reorganize the local government of the city of New York," so that such bill shall, as a law, conform to the intent of the legislature.

Passed April 29, 1873; three-fifths being present.

The People of the State of New York, represented in Senate and Assembly, do enact as follows:

SECTION 1. Nothing contained in the bill or act entitled "An act to reorganize the local government of the city of New York," passed at this session of the legislature, shall affect any right heretofore accrued or liability heretofore incurred, or prevent the indictment, or prosecution under indictments found or to be found, of any person or persons, for any offense or offenses heretofore committed, and all such rights, liabilities and offenses shall remain subject to redress, enforcement and punishment in like manner as if the acts so repealed as aforesaid had remained in full force.

Indictments and prosecutions.

SEC. 2. This act shall take effect immediately.

GENERAL INDEX.

A

	PAGE.
Absent members, authority to compel attendance	5
Abstract of meetings of Board of Aldermen, and all departments, to be published in the City Record	9, 82

ACCOUNTS OF—

city and county, mode of keeping	14, 25
city treasury, annual close and examination of	29
Acting Mayor, powers of	15

ADVERTISING—

for departments to be in the City Record	66, 67
in English and German papers	83, 84, 127
Aldermen—see BOARD OF.	
Aldermen at Large	3, 106
Annual salaries of officers	96
Appointments and removals to be published	82
Appropriations, unexpended, may be transferred	92, 114, 129
Areas	13
Armories and drill-rooms	127
Arrests by police force	40, 41
Ashes and garbage	12

ASSESSMENTS—

PAGE.

    when valid and binding............ 23

    Bureau for Collection of............................ 26, 27

    for all street improvements, to be collected only once ... 114

Assistant Aldermen—see BOARD OF.

Attorneys, by whom appointed...... 32

Auction—see PUBLIC AUCTION.

Auditing Bureau, Department of Finance................ 26

Awnings and awning-posts................................... 12

B

BANKS—

    weekly statement of city deposits to be made by........ 28

    how chosen... 30

Banners... 13

Bids—see CONTRACT.

Board of Assistant Aldermen, abolished after January 1, 1875.. 2, 106

BOARD OF ALDERMEN—

    legislative powers vested in........................1, 2, 4, 10

    term of office of, and when elected.....................2, 3, 105

    Aldermen for eighth senate district, and twenty-third
       and twenty-fourth wards.... 2

    Aldermen at Large................................. 3, 106

    vacancy in.. 3, 106

    boards to meet in separate chambers.................. 4

    officers of, how elected.............................. 4, 8

    Alderman not to act as magistrate in any judicial
       proceeding..................................... 5

    expulsion of members of............................ 5, 109

BOARD OF ALDERMEN—

PAGE.

occasional and stated meetings........ 5

legislation of, to be by resolution and ordinance......... 5

proceedings of, in case of veto by Mayor............... 6

legislative acts may originate in either board........... 7

abstract of meetings to be published in City Record..... 9, 10

President of, may act as Mayor...................... 15

to investigate and report upon the annual estimate...... 89

meetings of Board........................... 110

salaries of members....... 115

BOARD OF—

Commissioners of Sinking Fund..................... 73

Education.......................................24, 88, 111

Estimate and Apportionment, how organized........... 88

to make an annual estimate, and submit the same to
Common Council.............................. 88, 89

may authorize the issue of stock.................... 91

may transfer unexpended appropriations..........91, 92, 129

may revise and alter the annual estimate for 1873..... 127

may revise and alter the annual estimate for 1874....127, 130

Street Opening and Improvement, organization and
duties of...................................... 74

Supervisors, duties of (see SUPERVISORS).............. 90. 128

BOARDS—

powers and duties of, as defined in Article XVI........ 64

to keep a record and publish weekly statement of transactions............................ 82

Bribery in all forms punished as felony 70

Buildings—see DEPARTMENT.

Bulkheads... 64

Bureaus—

	Page.
may be consolidated	22
list of their powers and duties	26
in Law Department	33
in Department of Public Works	50
in Department of Charities and Correction.	54
in Fire Department	55
in Health Department	58
chiefs of, in any department, to give information whenever required by taxpayer	78, 80

C

Cabmen, cartmen, and car-drivers	13
Canvass of votes	87
Certificate of appointment	68
Chairman of Finance Committee to be member of Sinking Fund Commission	73

Chamberlain, City—

appointment and duties of	27, 30, 116
may select the banks or trust companies in which to deposit the city funds	30, 117
salary allowed to, in lieu of fees and commissions	31, 73
commissions received by, credited to the Sinking Fund	31, 32
may appoint his deputy and other officer	31
to be a member of Board of Commissioners of Sinking Fund	72, 73
to make weekly statement to Mayor and Comptroller	31, 117

PAGE.

Charters, Dongan and Montgomerie......................... 102

City Marshals.. 68, 99

City officers not to hold State or Federal offices.............. 94

CITY RECORD—

to be published under contract...................82, 83, 84

appointment of supervisor and officers of............82, 83, 86

to publish only official reports, advertisements of departments, etc..................................... 83

abstracts of minutes of Board of Aldermen to be
published in.................................... 9

to be verified by Comptroller, bound and recorded
quarterly...................................... 10

contents of, to be accepted as official in judicial
proceedings 10

approved ordinances and resolutions to be published in.. 14

ten per cent. on contract for publishing reserved........ 85

CITY RECORD TO PUBLISH—

quarterly statement of Mayor........................ 17

quarterly reports from the various departments........ 20

advertisements of lost property...................... 44, 45

bids and proposals for departments.................... 66

notices for street openings and improvements........... 75

quarterly reports of Commissioners of Accounts........ 78

annual statement of Comptroller..................... 79

brief abstracts of the weekly business of all departments 82

an annual list of all officers and subordinates of
departments................................... 86

revised annual estimates of Board of Apportionment 89, 90

Civil and consulting engineers............................ 94, 114

CLERK OF BOARD OF ALDERMEN—

PAGE.

to be Clerk of Common Council........................4, 8, 110

to be Clerk of Board of Supervisors.................... 8, 110

to prepare abstract of meetings of Board for publication.   9

CLERKS—

and other officers, to be officers of the Board of
Supervisors 8, 110

salaries of...   9

in departments, how appointed and removed........... 21, 22 .

in office of Chamberlain............................. 31, 117

prohibited from being interested in contracts...........   72

may be summarily examined on affidavit...............   80

COMMISSIONERS OF ACCOUNTS—

appointment of..................................... 77, 78

shall annually examine the accounts of the city treasury.   29

to make quarterly and other reports..................   78

salaries of... 97, 115

Commissioners of Estimate and Assessment in street matters...   76

Commissioners of the Sinking Fund........................   73

Commissioners of various departments—see DEPARTMENT.

COMMON COUNCIL—

enumeration of powers of........................... 10–14

prohibited from imposing taxes, creating debts, etc......   14

see BOARD OF ALDERMEN.

Compensation—see SALARY.

COMPTROLLER —

                                                  PAGE.

to verify and record, quarterly, bound copies of the City Record.......... 10

relative to term of office of.......... 17

powers and duties of, as head of the Finance Department.......... 22, 25

to be member of Board of Commissioners of Sinking Fund.......... 73

to be member of Board for Street Opening and Improvement.......... 74

when authorized to borrow moneys on bonds, etc........ 77

at end of each fiscal year to publish a financial statement.......... 79

to furnish to each department a weekly statement of its accounts.......... 111

Consolidation of city and county...........107, 108

Consulting engineers, when may hold more than one office..... 94

Contested elections, costs of, how defrayed................. 93

Contractor to give security................. 66

CONTRACTS—

not binding without an appropriation... 23

for lighting streets and avenues...................... 51

to be made and published by the respective departments.......... 65

to be executed and filed in duplicate................. 67

not to be awarded to persons in arrears to the city...... 70

corporation officers not to be interested in............. 72

when declared void................. 72

CONTRACTS —

                                                       PAGE.

for publishing the City Record.................... 82–84

for printing and stationery.............84, 85, 87, 114, 125

separate contract may be made for maps, engravings,

    etc 85

for removal of contents of sinks and privies............ 122

CORPORATION, CITY—

    organization of..................................... 1

    legislative powers of, how vested..................... 1

    executive powers of, how vested..................... 14

    county of New York, consolidated with.............. 107

Corporation Attorney 33

COUNSEL TO CORPORATION—

    appointment of, by Mayor........................... 17

    head of the Law Department 32, 33

    salary allowed to, in lieu of fees..................... 33, 96

Corps of Sappers and Miners in Fire Department............121, 122

Counsel in case of contested election...................... 93

County of New York, acts to consolidate with the City of New

    York..107, 108, 130

County buildings, act for completion of.................... 124

Croton water, supply and revenues of.................... 49, 50

D

PAGE.

Denominational or religious schools 54, 111

DEPARTMENT OF—

    Buildings:

        quarterly report of business of, to be made to
        Mayor   21

        appointment and duties of officers of............17, 62, 112

        act defining duties of Commissioners of...   124

    Docks............................ .... 20, 64

    Finance—see COMPTROLLER.

    Fire—see FIRE DEPARTMENT.

    Health—see HEALTH DEPARTMENT.

    Law—see LAW DEPARTMENT.

    Police—see POLICE DEPARTMENT.

    Public Charities and Correction......................   53

    Public Parks...................................... 60, 119

    Public Works..................... .... 48, 49

        officers, their powers and duties.................... 48–51

        bureaus of.. 49–51

        act defining duties of Commissioners of, in repavement
        of streets, etc....................................   120

Departmental estimates..................................   89

DEPARTMENTS, HEADS OF—

    their appointment and removal.....................17, 18, 19

    to appoint chiefs of bureaus, clerks and employees......   21

    may consolidate two or more bureaus.................   22

    not to be interested in any contract or work...........   72

    to furnish certified copies of all papers or accounts
    requested   78

DEPARTMENTS, HEADS OF—

	PAGE.
summary examination of, on affidavit	80
to publish weekly abstracts in the City Record	82, 86
salaries of	96

Deputy Clerks of Board of Aldermen 8

Deputy Comptroller 25

Docks, Department of 18, 64

Drill officers in Fire Department 121

Duties of Officers—see POWERS AND DUTIES.

E

Education, provisional estimates for .... 88.

ELECTION—

of Aldermen and Aldermen at Large	2
increase of vacancy	3
of Mayor	15
of temporary Chairman of Board	16
of city officers, provisions of law in relation to	74
election canvass to be published in City Record	87
contested, cost of	93
booths, under control of police force	43

Encroachments and street obstructions 11

Estimates, provisional 88, 89, 90

Estimates for 1873 and 1874, revision of 126, 127, 130

Executive power of the Coporation 14

Extension line of piers and bulkheads 64

Expenditures by Board of Aldermen 7, 9

Expenses in publishing City Record 83

Expiration of terms of office 98

Expulsion from legislative boards 109

F

FEES—

PAGE.

    in offices of city government, abolished............ 68

    in bureau of Law Department........................ 33

    received by all city officers to be paid weekly in city

        treasury 69

    of City Chamberlain................................ 117

Finance Department—see COMPTROLLER.

Finances, city, Mayor to make annual statement of........... 16

Financial statement to be published before each charter

        election... 79

FIRE DEPARTMENT—

    Commissioners and Bureaus......................20, 55, 57

    government and discipline of........................ 56

    Commissioners of, to publish quarterly report in City

        Record 21

    rules, discipline, orders and fines.................... 56

    relief fund.. 56

    membership, qualifications for...................... 57, 112

    general powers of Commissioners.................. ... 57

    repeal of former acts relating to...................... 100

    organization of corps of sappers and miners, and duties..121, 122

    appointment of drill officer......................... 121

    shall establish depot for explosives.................. 122

Fire Marshals... 55

Flags or placards in streets 13

Funds held by County Treasurer.......................... 108

G

PAGE.

General provisions, powers, and limitations... 64

General powers of the departments.......................... 99

H

Heads of Departments—see DEPARTMENTS, HEADS OF.

HEALTH DEPARTMENT—

    organization of.................................... 20, 57

    bureaus of.. 58

    may appoint an attorney, with salary.................. 58

    shall publish a "sanitary code," and punish violations of 58, 59

    powers conferred by former acts merged in the........ 60, 112

    shall make new contract for removal of contents of sinks

        and privies.................................. 122

House of Detention for Witnesses........... 41

I

Indictment, act continuing in force laws relating to........... 132

Inquisitions of coroners, to be recorded..................... 58

Inspection and sealing of weights and measures.............. 13

Inspector of Street Cleaning.............................. 46

Insurance Fund, Police................................... 101

Intoxication, fighting, etc., power of Common Council to

    regulate.................................... 13

J

	PAGE.
Junk dealers, pedlers, etc., Common Council shall license......	13
Jury and military duty, exemption from.....................	41
Justices of the Supreme Court, trials for malfeasance in office to be brought before............................	80, 81
Justices of the district courts, salaries of, fixed...............	98, 116

L

LAW DEPARTMENT—

organization of.....................................	20, 32
Counsel to Corporation, appointment and term of office of.	21, 33
bureaus in.............	33
salary allowed to counsel in lieu of fees................	33. 96
Legislative acts of Common Council to be approved by Mayor..	5
Legislative powers of Corporation	1
Licenses, authority to grant, vested in office of Mayor.........	13
Liens on premises for water rents	52, 53

M

Manual, City, not to be printed at public expense.............	86
Market property, conditions of sale or lease of...............	73
Markets excepted from sale................................	113

MAYOR—

veto by..	6
may approve and sign certain portions of an ordinance..	6, 7
not to approve any ordinance until after expiration of three days.............................	9

10

MAYOR—

                                                                     PAGE.

first election of...................... 15

when President of Board may act as................... 15, 16

general duties of.................................... 16

may appoint his clerks and subordinates.............. 17

shall nominate heads of departments................. 17

how removed.. 19

may remove heads of departments, for cause.......... 19

may fill vacancy for balance of term in Board of
    Aldermen........... .... 20, 119

to be a member of Board of Street Opening and
    Improvement.................................. 74

amendment to act prescribing election, etc., of........ 110

amendment to act prescribing time allowed in approval
    and return of official papers...................... 110

Meetings of Board of Aldermen............................ 110

Meetings of Board of Supervisors.......................... 90

Messages and reports, number of copies to be printed, limited.. 86

Meter, water, bills for use of, a lien on premises.............. 52, 53

Metropolitan police and fire districts, repeal of provisions of an
    act providing for................................. 100

Monthly statement, Chamberlain to make.................... 29

N

Notice to be given to Comptroller on recovery of judgment.... 77

Notices for street improvements to be published.............. 75

O

PAGE.

Oath of office to be taken by all persons in employ of city government 68

Oath to be taken in settlement of account.................... 23, 38

Officers under city government, summary examination of...... 80

Officers and heads of departments, salaries of 96–98

Official hours of business to be published.................... 87

Opening of streets................................ 11

ORDINANCE OR RESOLUTION—

> to be submitted to Mayor for approval...............6, 9, 110
>
> proceedings in case of veto of........................ 6
>
> may originate in either board........................ 7
>
> to be published in City Record before final approval..... 9
>
> power vested in Board of Aldermen to modify or repeal.. 10
>
> adopted under acts passed in 1870, to continue in force.. 102

P

PAY-ROLLS—

> warrants for amount of, may be payable to a single officer 24, 111
>
> of Board of Education............................... 24, 111

POLICE DEPARTMENT—

> to make quarterly report to Mayor.................... 20, 21
>
> appointments and removals vested in four commissioners...................................... 34
>
> appointments and removals to be published in City Record 36, 37

POLICE DEPARTMENT—

PAGE.

    Commissioners of Police, term of office of.....18, 34, 98, 99, 118

        powers and duties of....... .... 34, 48

        term of office of, in 1873 98

    dismissals... 41

    House of Detention for Witnesses..................... 41

    military assistance when board may demand............ 37

    police surgeons..................................... 43

    President of Board................................... 17

    rules and regulations................................ 40

    salary and pay of officers and members of............. 36

    special patrolmen, and powers of..................... 37

    station houses...................................... 39

    trial of witnesses................................... 38

    police insurance fund............................... 101

POWERS AND DUTIES OF—

    Acting Mayor....................................... 15

    Board of Aldermen or Common Council........4, 10, 11–14, 106

        . 108, 120

    Board of Aldermen, denied judicial powers............ 5

    Board of Commissioners of Sinking Fund.............. 73

    Board of Police..................................45, 46, 118

    Board of Street Opening............................. 74

    Board of Estimate and Apportionment......88, 92, 126, 127, 131

    City Chamberlain................................27 32, 116

    Clerks of Board of Aldermen........................89, 110

    Commissioner of Public Works.....................51–53, 95

    Commissioners of Public Parks....................... 119

    Common Council................................10, 14, 65

    Comptroller and Finance Department..............22–25, 111

Powers and Duties of—

PAGE.

Counsel to Corporation, and officers.................... 32, 33

Department of Public Parks......................... 60

Deputy Commissioner of Public Works............... 48

Deputy Comptroller............................... 25, 26

Fire Commissioners...........................55, 57, 121

Fire Marshal 55

Heads of departments..........................21, 22, 88

Health Department.............................. 112, 122

Inspector of Combustibles........................... 55

Justice, in summary examination of officers............ 81

Mayor.. 15–20

Metropolitan Board of Health, as merged in Health
  Department..........................59, 60, 110, 112

Police Commissioners...........................45, 46, 118

Police force.. 40

Sanitary Superintendent............................. 58

Special patrolmen................................... ·37

Superintendent of Buildings.................62, 112, 113, 124

Supervisor of City Record........................... 86

Supervisors, county.....................90, 107, 126, 128, 131

Various boards and officers of city government......... 64

President of –

Board of Aldermen, and salary.................. ..... 4, 115

each department, entitled to seat in Board of Aldermen. 4

Department of Public Parks and Public Works, Mayor
  not authorized to appoint........................ 17

Board of Police, to be members of Health Department.. 57

Department of Taxes and Assessments................ 63

PRESIDENT OF—

PAGE.

Board of Aldermen, to be member of Board of
Estimate. etc.................................... 88

Printing, City Record—see CITY RECORD.

PRINTING AND STATIONERY—

shall be furnished under contract..................... 84

proposals and specifications for, to be filed 84, 85

blanks and blank-books.............................. 84

separate contracts for wood-cuts, maps, etc............ 85

judgments against city for, not valid unless done under
contract 85

messages, reports, etc., limitation of copies............ 86

may be ordered and furnished without contract.....87, 114, 125

see also CITY RECORD.

Proceedings in case of veto................................ 6

Property to be sold at auction............................. 67

Proposals for contracts to be advertised...................... 66

Provisional estimates. what to contain in detail.............. 88, 89

Public Administrator, bureau of........................... 33

Public amusements....................................... 13

PUBLIC AUCTION—

when Property Clerk of Police Department may sell at.. 45

all property of the Departments to be sold at........... 67, 68

proceeds of sales to be deposited with Chamberlain...... 67

Commissioners of Sinking Fund may sell or lease market
property at..................................... 73, 113

Public fountains....................................... 14

Public Works—see DEPARTMENT OF.

Q

QUARTERLY REPORTS—

PAGE.

from departments, to be published.................... 21

from Counsel to Corporation......................... 33

QUORUM—

majority of any board to constitute a................. 64

of Board of Aldermen.............................. 4

of Board of Commissioners of Estimate and Assessment.. 77

R

Religious or denominational school..................... 111

REMOVALS—

heads of departments.............................. 19

Deputy Comptroller............................... 25

to be published in City Record...................... 82

REPAVING OF STREETS—

only one assessment for........................... 95, 114

assessments on adjoining property for................ 114

act providing for a more uniform system for.......... 120

to be done by Department of Public Works............ 120

costs of, to be inserted in annual tax levy............. 95, 120

Resolution—see ORDINANCE.

Richmond, County of................................. 47

S

Salary, in lieu of fees, commissions, etc., for all city officers... 68

SALARY OF—

Attorney... 68

Chamberlain.................................31, 96, 117

chief officers under city government, list of............ 96

SALARY OF—

                                                             PAGE.

    clerks... 8

    Commissioners of Accounts....................... .... 78, 115

    deputy clerks....................................... 8

    Drill Officer of Fire Department...................... 121

    justices of district courts............................. 98, 116

    members of Board of Aldermen...................... 115

SALARY OF—

    officers of the city government, to be fixed by Board of
        Apportionment................................. 70

    officers of the city government, to be fixed by the
        Common Council..................... 70

    policemen... 36

    President of Board of Aldermen...................... 115

    presidents and heads of departments.................. 96

    subordinates in departments......................... 98, 115

    Superintendent of Police........................... 98, 115

Salaries in detail, under section 116........................ 96, 97

SANITARY CODE—

    Board of Health to revise and adopt.................. 58, 59

    additions may be made to and published............... 59

    penalties for violations of........................... 59

Sanitary Superintendent... 58

Sappers and miners in Fire Department.....................121, 122

Sinking Fund, Board of Commissioners of................... 73, 74

Sinks and privies. contract for removal of contents of........ 122

Special patrolmen, and duties of........................... 37

Special contingencies, excluded from annual estimates........ 129

	PAGE.
Stated and occasional meetings	111
Stationery and blanks, proposals for printing	84
Station-houses and sub-stations	39
Stolen property, taken by police force, how disposed of	43, 44

STREETS—

powers of Common Council to regulate	10, 11, 12
Inspector of Street Cleaning	46
duties of Commissioner of Public Works as to obstructions, repairs, or improvements in	49, 50, 120
avenues, boulevards, etc., above Fifty-ninth street	53
pavement of, by assessments, how affected	95, 115, 120
repavement of, cost of, to be by general tax	95, 114, 115, 120
Street Cleaning Bureau, under control of Police Department	46

SUBORDINATES—

not to receive as large salaries as chiefs	98
in departments, changes of and annual list to be published	86
Subpœnas, Police Board may issue	38
Summary examinations of all elected or appointed officers	80
Supervisor of City Record, duties and powers of	82, 83, 86

SUPERVISORS, BOARD OF—

clerks of Board of Aldermen to be clerks of	8, 110
organization and powers of	90, 91
transfer of liabilities and duties of, to Board of Aldermen	107, 108
empowered to raise the revised estimates for 1873 and 1874	126, 128, 131

SUPERINTENDENT OF—

PAGE.

Buildings..................................62, 97, 98, 112, 113

Markets 27

Police, duties and salary of.......... ...34, 42, 46, 98, 99, 115

Repair yard in Fire Department, term of office of...... 99

Sanitary, of Health Department....................... 58

Superintendents of bureaus of public works................. 50, 51

Surgeons of police, appointment of........................ 35, 99

T

Tax payers, rights of, to examine books of Finance Department, etc... 80

TAXES—

Board of Supervisors authorized to raise.......90, 91, 126, 128,
129, 131

Bureau for collection of............................ 27

Common Council prohibited from imposing............ 14

Corporation officers not to be interested in property
sold for.. 72

Taxes and Assessments, Department of..................... 21, 63

Treasurer of Board of Police, to give bond, with surety........ 42

U

Unexpended balances of appropriations, transfer of...92, 111, 114. 129

V

VACANCIES—

in Board of Aldermen............................... 3, 106

in office of Mayor.................................. 16

in departments, Mayor authorized to fill.............. 20

VETO—

		PAGE.
by Mayor, to be entered on minutes of Board		3, 6
proceedings and vote in case of		6
Vote, official, trial and penalty for violation of intent of		71
Votes, election, canvass of, to be published in City Record		87

W

Wages, to be paid as per pay-roll	111
Water-meters, a lien on premises	52
Water-pipes, laying of, etc	50
Water-rents, bureau for collection of	26

WEEKLY STATEMENT—

banks and trust companies to transmit	28
City Chamberlain to transmit to Mayor	31
from all departments to be published in City Record	82
Comptroller directed to furnish to heads of departments	111
Witnesses, in case of summary examination	81

LAWS OF THE STATE

AFFECTING INTERESTS IN THE

Ⓒity and Ⓒounty of Ⓝew Ⓨork,

PASSED BY THE

LEGISLATURE OF 1876.

BOARD OF ALDERMEN,

MAY 11, 1876.

New York:

MARTIN B. BROWN, PRINTER AND STATIONER,

201, 203 & 205 WILLIAM STREET.

BOARD OF ALDERMEN,

MAY 11, 1876.

The following resolution was adopted:

Resolved, That the Clerk of the Common Council be and he is hereby authorized and directed to cause one thousand copies of all laws relating particularly to this city, passed at the late session of the Legislature, to be printed in the usual manner, in document form, for the use of the Mayor, Common Council, and Departments; the expense of procuring certified copies of such laws, which shall not exceed the sum of one hundred dollars, to be paid from the appropriation for " City Contingencies" by the Comptroller.

FRANCIS J. TWOMEY,
Clerk.

INDEX.

—— ◆ ——

City Government—Miscellaneous Laws relating to.

PAGE.

Chapter   73.   Ferry from Grand street, New York, to Grand street, Brooklyn, act authorizing sale of lease of.   3

Chapter 103.   Assessments for local improvements, act relating to the payment of.............................   5

Chapter 208.   Assessment for taxes, act to extend the time for making.   21

Chapter 212.   Frauds upon the treasury of the city, act making provision for the claims and expenses of conducting suits, etc., growing out of..................   27

Chapter 213.   New York Infant Asylum, act to amend an act to incorporate the..............................   28

Chapter 274.   Arrears of taxes, act in relation to...............   30

Chapter 429.   Armories and drill-rooms, act to provide for payment for the use and occupation of............   51

Courts—Laws and Matters pertaining to.

Chapter   21.   First and Second Judicial Districts, act to alter....   3

Chapter 130.   Notaries Public, act to provide for the appointment of an additional number of.   7

Chapter 136.   Marine Court, act to amend an act in relation to the jurisdiction of, etc.   8

PAGE.

Chapter 199. Court of General Sessions, act in relation to........ 20

Chapter 205. Clerks, etc., of the several Courts of Record, act in relation to................................... 21

Chapter 209. Court-house in the Third Judicial District, act to provide for the completion of................. 22

Chapter 316. Judgments entered upon forfeited recognizances, act relative to.............................. 37

Chapter 356. Proceedings to recover possession of lands for non-payment of rent, act in relation to............ 38

Chapter 409. Act to enable the Court of General Sessions to appoint an Interpreter......................... 46

Chapter 413. Marine Court, act in relation to the Clerks, Officers, and Attendants of................ 49

Department of Public Parks—Matters pertaining to.

Chapter 139. American Museum of Natural History and the Metropolitan Museum of Art, act in relation to the powers and duties of the Commissioners of the Department of Public Parks in connection with...................................... 9

Chapter 411. Act to provide for the surveying and mapping out of the territory comprised in the Twenty-third and Twenty-fourth Wards.................... 47

Department of Public Works—Matters pertaining to.

Chapter 169. Public baths, act to provide for the construction and maintenance of four additional............ 17

Chapter 432. Act to provide for a further supply of water for the new wards..... 53

Chapter 433. Act to amend an act to provide a further supply of pure and wholesome water.................... 56

Educational Matters—Laws relating to.

PAGE.

Chapter 296. School property in the town of Westchester, act to provide for the payment of amount due for..... 33

Chapter 372. Act to amend an act to secure to children the benefits of an elementary education............ 39

Chapter 434. Claims for repairs, printing, labor, etc., in and about public school buildings, act to provide for the audit and payment of........................ 57

Harbor and River Frontage—Laws relating to.

Chapter 147. Harlem river and Spuyten Duyvel creek, act granting the right of way necessary for the improvement of, etc................. 10

Chapter 188. Improvement of lands on the Harlem river, act to fix the time for 19

Chapter 376. Act to prevent the deposit of refuse in the Hudson river, etc..................................... 43

Chapter 414. Act to amend an act to establish regulations for the port of New York............................ 5

Local and Street Improvements.

Chapter 210. Opening, widening, and extending of streets. etc., act to repeal an act in relation to............. 23

Chapter 436. Act to amend and act to provide for the surveying laying out, etc., of certain portions of the city... 59

Chapter 447. Riverside avenue and park, act in relation to....... 60

Miscellaneous Acts.

Chapter 1. Act to prevent persons appearing disguised and armed, act to amend......................... 1

Chapter 16. Animals, act to prevent injury to................ 2

PAGE.

Chapter 116. Public amusement, places of, act to amend an act
              to regulate   6

Chapter 148. Bridget Porter, act to release certain real estate to. 16

Chapter 211. James B. Taylor, act for the relief of the creditors
              of.   24

Chapter 275. Cornelius Flynn, act for the relief of.............   31

Chapter 291. Commissioners of Emigration, act making an appro-
              priation to enable them to perform their duties...   32

Chapter 300. Patrick McCabe, act for the relief of.   36

Chapter 1.

AN ACT to amend chapter three of the laws of one thousand eight hundred and forty-five, entitled " An act to prevent persons appearing disguised and armed."

Passed January 20, 1876 ; three-fifths being present.

The People of the State of New York, represented in Senate and Assembly, do enact as follows :

SECTION 1. Section six, of chapter three, of the laws of eighteen hundred and forty-five, entitled " An act to prevent persons appearing disguised and armed," passed January twenty-eighth, eighteen hundred and forty-five, is hereby amended so as to read as follows :

§ 6. Every assemblage in public houses or other places of three or more persons disguised as aforesaid, is hereby declared to be unlawful, and every individual so disguised present thereat, shall be deemed guilty of a misdemeanor, and upon conviction be punished by imprisonment in the county jail not exceeding one year, provided that nothing contained in this act shall be held or construed as prohibiting or as rendering unlawful any peaceable assemblage for any masquerade or fancy dress ball or entertainment, or any assemblage therefor of persons masked, or as prohibiting or rendering unlawful the wearing of masks, fancy dresses, or any other disguise, by persons on their way to, or returning from, such ball or other entertainment ; and provided, also, that in the cities of this state permission be first obtained from the police authorities of the said cities for the holding or giving of any such masquerade or fancy

[sidenote: Persons permitted to assemble in masquerade or fancy dress.]

dress ball or entertainment therein, under such regulations as may be prescribed by the said police authorities.

§ 2. All acts and parts of acts inconsistent with this act are hereby repealed.

§ 3. This act shall take effect immediately.

Chapter 16.

AN ACT to prevent injury to animals in the city of New York.

Passed February 8, 1876; three-fifths being present.

The People of the State of New York, represented in Senate and Assembly, do enact as follows:

Throwing of metal, glass, etc., upon any street deemed a misdemeanor.

SECTION 1. Every person who shall willfully throw, expose, or place, or who shall willfully cause or procure to be thrown, exposed or placed, in or upon any street, highway, or public place in the city of New York, open for the passage of animals, any nails, pieces of metal, glass, or other substance or thing which might main, wound, lame, cut or otherwise injure any animal, shall be guilty of a misdemeanor.

Sprinkling salt or saltpeter upon any street.

§ 2. Every person who shall throw, expose, or place, or who shall cause or procure to be thrown, exposed or placed, in or upon any such street, highway or public place except upon the curves, crossings or switches of railroad tracks, any salt, saltpeter or other substance for the purpose of dissolving any snow or ice which may have fallen or been deposited thereon, shall be guilty of a misdemeanor.

§ 3. This act shall take effect at the expiration of ten days after its passage.

Chapter 24.

AN ACT to alter the first and second judicial districts of the state as established by chapter two hundred and forty-one of the laws of eighteen hundred and forty-seven, entitled "An act to divide the state into judicial districts," so as to conform the same to the boundaries of the city of New York and of the county of Westchester as now constituted by law.

Passed February 21, 1876 ; three-fifths being present.

The People of the State of New York, represented in Senate and Assembly, do enact as follows:

SECTION 1. The first judicial district of the state shall consist of the city of New York, as the same has been constituted by law since the first day of January, eighteen hundred and seventy-four. The second judicial district shall consist of the counties of Richmond, Suffolk, Queens, Kings, Westchester, as the same has been constituted by law since the first day of January, eighteen hundred and seventy-four, Orange, Rockland, Putnam and Dutchess.

Establishing the first and second judicial districts.

§ 2. This act shall take effect immediately.

Chapter 73.

AN ACT to authorize the commissioners of the sinking fund of the city of New York to sell at public auction the lease of the ferry from Grand street, in the city of New York, to Grand street, in the city of Brooklyn.

Passed March 24, 1876 ; three-fifths being present.

The People of the State of New York, represented in Senate and Assembly, do enact as follows:

SECTION 1. The commissioners of the sinking fund of the city of New York are hereby authorized and directed,

within twenty days from the passage of this act, to adver-
tise in three of the daily newspapers having the largest
circulation, published in the city of New York, and one
newspaper published in the city of Brooklyn, for six days
in each of said newspapers, a notice of the sale by public
auction at the expiration of said six days, to the highest
bidder, at a time and place to be designated therein, in
the said city of New York, of the lease for a period of ten
years, of the full and absolute purchase and right, to run
maintain, operate, and use with the franchises, the ferry
from Grand street in said city, to Grand street in the city
of Brooklyn, together with the docks, slips, and facilities,
now or heretofore used for the purpose of a ferry.

§ 2. The said commissioners of the sinking fund shall,
within ten days after such sale, execute and deliver to the
highest bidder as aforesaid, a lease for the term of ten
years from the date thereof, of the said ferry, docks, slips,
and facilities; such lease to contain proper and reasonable
restrictions as to the kind of boats to be used, the time of
running the same, the kind of buildings to be erected for
the accommodation of passengers at each terminus of said
ferry, and the rate or rates of fare to be charged for the
conveying of passengers, goods, and merchandise, vehicles,
animals, and all other articles which may be conveyed
over such ferry, all of which are to be specified and determined by the said commissioners of the sinking fund.
But such fare or charges shall not at any time exceed the
fare or charges now made and collected by the Houston
Street Ferry Company for similar services performed by
them.

§ 3. Such lease shall also contain a suitable provision
for the payment to such lessee or his assigns at the end of
said term, by any other person or persons to whom such
franchise and property shall thereafter be leased, of the
value of the buildings, bridges, and racks which shall have

been provided by him or them for the operation of said franchises under such lease; such value to be ascertained by arbitration and appraised in a manner to be provided in and by such lease.

§ 4. All acts or parts of acts conflicting with this act, are hereby repealed.

§ 5. This act shall take effect immediately.

———

Chapter 103.

AN ACT relating to the payment of assessments for local improvements in the City of New York.

Passed April 7, 1876; three-fifths being present.

The People of the State of New York, represented in Senate and Assembly, do enact as follows :

SECTION 1. All assessments for local improvements in the city of New York, confirmed prior to the first day of January, eighteen hundred and seventy-six, and which, at the time of the passage of this act, have been returned to the clerk of arrears for collection, may be paid at the option of the person liable to pay the same, in three equal installments, as follows: The first installment on or before the thirty-first day of December, eighteen hundred and seventy-six; the second installment on or before the thirty-first day of December, eighteen hundred and seventy-seven, and the third installment on or before the thirty-first day of December, eighteen hundred and seventy-eight, with interest at the rate of eight per cent. per annum thereon. But nothing contained in this section shall prohibit the person liable to pay an assessment from paying the whole amount of such assessment in one payment, if he may so desire.

Payment by installments, time specified for the.

§ 2. No lien shall be enforced by said city for payment of said assessments, or any part or portion thereof, if payment of the same is made as hereinbefore provided.

Failure to make the necessary payments.

§ 3. Nothing herein contained shall in any way affect the rights or remedies of the said city in relation to said assessments and the recovery thereof, except that the payments may be made as herein provided. Upon a failure in the payment of said assessments, as herein provided, the privileges by this statute confirmed, shall be forfeited, and the said assessments, or the balance remaining unpaid, may, upon such forfeiture, be enforced, as if this statute had never been passed.

§ 4. This act shall take effect immediately.

Chapter 116.

AN ACT to amend chapter one hundred and fifty-eight of the laws of eighteen hundred and seventy-five, entitled " An act to amend chapter eight hundred and thirty-six of the laws of eighteen hundred and seventy-two, entitled ' An act to regulate places of public amusement in the city of New York.'"

Passed April 11, 1876.

The People of the State of New York, represented in Senate and Assembly, do enact as follows :

SECTION 1. Section one of chapter one hundred and fifty-eight of the laws of eighteen hundred and seventy-five, entitled " An act to amend chapter eight hundred and thirty-six of the laws of eighteen hundred and seventy-two, entitled ' An act to regulate places of public amusement in the city of New York,'" is hereby amended so as to read as follows :

SECTION 1. Section nine of chapter eight hundred and thirty-six of the laws of eighteen hundred and seventy-two, entitled "An act to regulate places of public amusement in the city of New York," is hereby amended so as to read as follows:

§ 9. The provisions and requirements of said act shall not be held to apply to any building, hall, room, or rooms, in which only private theatricals, tableaux, and other exhibitions for charitable and religious purposes are given, nor to the manager or managers of exhibitions given by amateurs for the benefit of any church, mission, parish, or Sunday school, or for any other charitable or religious purpose, nor shall the same be held to apply to the masonic temple in New York, or the trustees of the masonic hall and asylum fund, so long as the revenues of said temple shall continue to be applied to the use of the masonic hall and asylum fund, or other charitable purpose.

Places of amusement exempt from the provisions of said act.

§ 2. This act shall take effect immediately.

Chapter 130.

AN ACT to provide for the appointment of an additional number of Notaries Public.

Passed April 18, 1876 ; three-fifths being present.

The People of the State of New York, represented in Senate and Assembly, do enact as follows :

SECTION 1. The governor is hereby authorized and empowered, by and with the advice and consent of the senate, to appoint in each county, except the city and county of New York, notaries public equal to ten for each assembly district, and in the said city and county two hundred and fifty notaries public, in addition to the number now

Notaries Public in the county of New York.

allowed by law; provided, however, that in each county which is a single assembly district the additional number of notaries public be fifteen.

§ 2. This act shall take effect immediately.

Chapter 136.

AN ACT to amend chapter four hundred and seventy-nine of the laws of eighteen hundred and seventy-five entitled " An act in relation to the jurisdiction of the marine court of the city of New York, and to the justices of said court."

Passed April 21, 1876; three-fifths being present.

The People of the State of New York, represented in Senate and Assembly, do enact as follows :

SECTION 1. The fifty-first section of chapter four hundred and seventy-nine of the laws of eighteen hundred and seventy-five, entitled " An act in relation to the jurisdiction of the marine court of the city of New York and to the justices of said court," is hereby amended by adding thereto the following sub-division :

Non-residents.

14. No person being a resident of the state of New York, who shall have a place of business in the city of New York, shall be deemed to be a non-resident under the provisions of this act.

§ 2. This act shall take effect immediately.

Chapter 139.

AN ACT in relation to the powers and duties of the board of commissioners of the department of public parks in connection with the American Museum of Natural History and the Metropolitan Museum of Art.

Passed April 22, 1876 ; three-fifths being present.

The People of the State of New York, represented in Senate and Assembly, do enact as follows :

SECTION 1. The board of commissioners of the department of public parks in the city of New York, is hereby authorized and directed to make and enter into a contract with the American Museum of Natural History for the occupation by it of the buildings erected or to be erected on that portion of the Central park in the city of New York, formerly known as Manhattan square in accordance with the second section of chapter two hundred and ninety of the laws of eighteen hundred and seventy-one, and chapter three hundred and fifty-one of the laws of eighteen hundred and seventy-five, and transferring thereto, and establishing and maintaining therein, its museum, library, and collections, and carrying out the objects and purposes of the said society.

Erection of the American Museum of Natural History.

§ 2. The board of commissioners of the department of public parks of the city of New York, is hereby authorized and directed to make and enter into a contract with the Metropolitan Museum of Art for the occupation by it of the buildings erected or to be erected on that portion of the Central park of the city of New York east of the old receiving reservoir, and bounded on the west by the drive, on the east by the Fifth avenue, on the south by a continuation of Eightieth street and on the north by a continuation of Eighty-fifth street, in accordance with the second section of chapter two hundred and ninety of the laws of eighteen hundred and seventy-one, and transferring

Occupation of by the Metropolitan Museum of Art.

thereto and establishing and maintaining therein its museum, library, and collections, and carrying out the objects and purposes of the said Museum of Art.

§ 3. This act shall take effect immediately.

Chapter 147.

AN ACT granting to the United States the right to acquire the right of way necessary for the improvement of the Harlem river and Spuyten Duyvel creek, from the North river to the East river through the Harlem Kills, and ceding jurisdiction over the same.

Passed April 22, 1876, by a two-third vote.

The People of the State of New York, represented in Senate and Assembly, do enact as follows:

Improve-
ment of the
Harlem river
and Spuyten
Duyvel
creek.

SECTION 1. The consent of the state of New York is hereby given to the improvement, by the United States, of the Harlem river and Spuyten Duyvel creek, from the North river to the East river through the Harlem Kills, and the United States may take and hold so much land and land underwater, with any improvements thereon, as may be necessary for the location, construction, and convenient use of the said improvement.

Petition for
the appoint-
ment of
commis-
sioners of
appraisal.

§ 2. In the absence of any agreement between the United States or its authorized agents and the owners of such lands in regard to the compensation therefor, the engineer in charge of the improvements for the United States, and any other authorized agent of the United States may verify and present a petition, in the name of the United States, praying for the appointment of commissioners of appraisal to the supreme court at any general or special term thereof, held in the first judicial district, which petition shall describe the real estate and material which the

United States seeks to acquire, and shall aver that such land is necessary for the construction and use of said improvement, and that the United States has not been able to acquire title thereto, and the reason of such inability. The petition must also state the names and places of residence, so far as the same can by reasonable diligence be ascertained, of the persons who own or hold, or claim to own or hold, estates or interests in the said real estate, and if any such persons are infants, their ages, as near as may be, shall be stated, and if any such persons are idiots or persons of unsound mind, or are unknown, the fact shall be stated, together with such allegations of liens or incumbrances, as the United States may see fit to make. A copy of such petition with notice of the time and place the same will be presented to the supreme court shall be served on all persons whose interests are to be affected by the proceedings, at least ten days prior to the presentation of the same to the said court.

Petition to contain names and places of business of the owners of real estate.

§ 3. On presenting such petition to the supreme court as aforesaid, with proof of service of a copy thereof, and notice as aforesaid, all persons whose estates or interests are to be affected by the proceedings, may show cause against granting the prayer of the petition, and may disprove any of the facts alleged in it. The court shall hear the proofs and allegations of the parties, and if no sufficient cause is shown against granting the prayer of the petition, it shall make an order for the appointment of five disinterested and competent persons who reside in the city of New York, commissioners to ascertain and appraise the compensation to be made to the owners, or persons interested in the real estate proposed to be taken for said improvement, and to fix the time and place for the first meeting of such commissioners.

Persons whose interests are to be affected by the proceedings may show cause against granting the prayer of the petition.

§ 4. The commissioners shall take and subscribe the oath prescribed by the twelfth article of the constitution.

Any one of them may issue subpœnas, administer oaths to witnesses, and any three of them may adjourn the proceedings before them, from time to time, in their discretion.

Whenever they meet, except by the appointment of the court, or pursuant to adjournment, they shall cause reasonable notice of such meetings to be given to the parties who are to be affected by their proceedings, or their attorney or agent. They shall view the premises described in the petition, and hear the proofs and allegations of the parties, and reduce the testimony, if any is taken by them, to writing, and after the testimony is closed in each case, and without any unnecessary delay and before proceeding to the examination of any other claim, a majority of them, all being present and acting, shall ascertain and determine the compensation which ought justly to be made to the party or parties owning or interested in the real estate appraised by them. They, or a majority of them, shall also determine and certify what sum ought to be paid to a general or special guardian or committee of an infant, idiot, or person of unsound mind, or to an attorney appointed by the court to attend to the interest of any unknown owner or party in interest, not personally served with notice of the proceedings, and who has not appeared for costs, expenses, and counsel fees. They shall make a report to the supreme court, signed by them, or a majority of them, of the proceedings before them, with the minutes of the testimony taken by them, if any.

§ 5. On such report being made by said commissioners, the United States shall give notice to the parties, or their attorneys, to be affected by the proceedings, according to the rules and practice of said court at a general or special term thereof for the confirmation of such report; and the court shall thereupon confirm such report, and shall make an order containing a recital of the substance of the proceedings in the matter of the appraisal, and a description of the real estate appraised for which compensation is to be made; and shall also direct to whom the money is to be paid, or in what bank, and in what manner it shall be deposited.

§ 6. A certified copy of the order, to be made as afore-said, shall be recorded at length in the county clerk's office of the city and county of New York, and thereupon the United States shall be entitled to enter upon, take posses-sion of, and use the said land for the purpose of said im-provement; and all persons who have been made parties to the proceedings shall be divested and barred of all right, estate, and interest in said land. All real estate acquired by the United States under and pursuant to the provisions of this act for the said improvements shall be deemed to be acquired for the public use. Within twenty days after the confirmation of the report of the commissioners, as pro-vided for in the fifth section of this act, either party may appeal, by notice in writing to the other, to the supreme court from the appraisal and report of the commissioners. Such appeal shall be heard by the supreme court at any general or special term thereof, on such notice thereof being given according to the rules and practice of said court. On the hearing of such appeal, the court may direct a new ap-praisal before the same or new commissioners in its dis-cretion; the second report shall be final and conclusive on all the parties interested. If the amount of the compensa-tion to be made is increased by the second report, the difference shall be a lien on the land appraised, and if the amount is diminished the difference shall be refunded by the party to whom the same may have been paid; and judgment therefor may be rendered by the court on the filing of the second report against the party liable to pay the same. Such appeal shall not affect the possession by the United States of the land appraised, and when the same is made by others than the United States it shall not be heard, except on a stipulation of the party appealing not to disturb such possession. If there are adverse and

(margin notes:) Certified copy to be filed in the office of the county clerk.

Appeal taken there-on.

Increase or decrease of compensa-tion by the second re-port.

conflicting claimants to the money, or any part of it to be paid as compensation for the real estate taken, the court may direct the money to be paid into said court, and may determine who is entitled to the same, and direct to whom the same shall be paid ; and may, in its discretion, order a reference to ascertain the facts on which such determination and order are to be made. The court shall appoint some competent attorney to appear for and protect the rights of any party in interest who is unknown, or whose residence is unknown, and who has not appeared in the proceedings by an attorney or agent. The court shall also have power at any time to amend any defect or informality in any of the special proceedings authorized by this act, as may be necessary, or to cause new parties to be added, and to direct such further notices to be given to any party in interest, as it deems proper, and also to appoint other commissioners in place of any who shall die, or refuse, or neglect to serve, or be incapable of serving.

Unknown parties to be represented by counsel.

§ 7. If at any time, after an attempt to acquire title by appraisal of damages or otherwise, it shall be found that the title thereby attempted to be acquired is defective, the United States may proceed anew to acquire or perfect such title in the same manner as if no appraisal had been made, and at any stage of such new proceedings the court may authorize the United States, if in possession, to continue in possession, and if not in possession, to take possession and use such real estate during the pendency, and until the final conclusion of such new proceedings ; and may stay all actions or proceedings against any agent of the United States on account thereof, on his giving security as the court may direct to pay the compensation therefor when finally ascertained ; and in every such case the party interested in such real estate may conduct the proceedings to a conclusion, if the United States delays or omits to prosecute the same.

Defective titles, how perfected.

§ 8. In case any title or interest in real estate required

by the United States for said improvement, shall be vested in any trustee not authorized to sell, release, and convey the same, or in any infant, idiot, or person of unsound mind, the supreme court shall have power, by a summary proceeding, on petition, to authorize and empower such trustee, or the general guardian or committee of such infant, idiot, or person of unsound mind, to sell and convey the same to the United States for said improvement on such terms as may be just; and in case any such infant, idiot, or person of unsound mind has no general guardian or committee, the said court may appoint a special guardian or committee for the purpose of making such sale, release, or conveyance, and may require such security from such general or special guardian or committee, as said court may deem proper. But before any conveyance or release, authorized by this section, shall be executed, the terms on which the same is to be executed, shall be reported to the court on oath, and if the court is satisfied that such terms are just to the party interested in such real estate, the court shall confirm the report, and direct the proper conveyance or release to be executed, which shall have the same effect as if executed by an owner of said land, having legal power to sell and convey the same.

Summary proceedings to acquire certain real estate.

§ 9. The jurisdiction of the state of New York, in and over the land and land under water required for said improvements, shall be and the same hereby is ceded to the United States, subject to the reservations and restrictions hereinafter mentioned.

Jurisdiction ceded to the United States.

§ 10. The said consent is given and the said jurisdiction ceded upon the express reservation to the state of New York of all the rights of said state over all bridges and tunnels now constructed, or hereafter to be constructed, in pursuance of existing laws, for the location thereof, by the department of public parks of the city of New York, over the said Harlem river, or Spuyten Duyvel creek, and upon

Jurisdiction over bridges and tunnels.

the express condition that the state of New York shall retain concurrent jurisdiction with the United States in and over the territory covered by said improvement as to all crimes committed thereon, and so far as that all civil and criminal process which may issue under the laws or authority of the state of New York, may be executed thereon in the same way and manner as if such consent had not been given or jurisdiction ceded, except so far as such process may affect the real or personal property of the United States.

Execution of civil and criminal process.

§ 11. The jurisdiction hereby ceded shall not vest in any respect as to any portion of said territory until the United States shall have acquired the title thereto by grant, or by virtue of the provisions of this act.

§ 12. The said property, when acquired by the United States, shall be, and continue forever thereafter, exonerated and discharged from all taxes, assessments, and other charges which may be levied or imposed under the authority of this state.

The United States discharged from all taxes and assessments.

§ 13. This act shall take effect immediately.

Chapter 148.

AN ACT to release to Bridget Porter the right, title, and interest of the people of the state of New York in and to certain real estate in the twenty-fourth ward of the city of New York.

Passed April 22, 1876, by a two-third vote.

The People of the State of New York, represented in Senate and Assembly, do enact as follows :

SECTION 1. All the estate, right, title, and interest of the people of the state of New York, of, in and to that certain lot or parcel of land, and the buildings thereon erected, situate, lying, and being in the twenty-fourth ward of the city of New York, designated by the number one hundred and sixty on a map, entitled "map of the Westchester property of Edward T. Young, Springhurst, New York," filed in the office of the register of New York on the twenty-fifth of October, eighteen hundred and seventy-three, and particularly described in the deed for the same, bearing date the second day of January, eighteen hundred and seventy-four, and executed by Edward T. Young and wife to Isaac Porter, which is recorded in the office of the register of the city of New York, in book one thousand two hundred and seventy-one of conveyances, page three hundred and ninety-six, on the fifth day of January, eighteen hundred and seventy-four, are hereby released to Bridget Porter, widow and sole devisee of said Isaac Porter, and to her heirs and assigns forever. And the said Bridget Porter is hereby authorized and empowered to sell, convey, mortgage, and devise the same in the manner, and with the like effect, as if she were a citizen of the United States of America.

§ 2. Nothing herein contained shall be construed to impair, release, or discharge any right, claim, or interest of any heir-at-law, devisee or grantee of the said Isaac Porter, or of any creditor by judgment, mortgage, or otherwise.

§ 3. This act shall take effect immediately.

Chapter 169.

AN ACT to provide for the construction and maintenance of four additional public baths in the city of New York.

Passed April 22, 1876; three-fifths present.

The People of the State of New York, represented in Senate and Assembly, do enact as follows:

SECTION 1. The mayor, aldermen and commonalty of

2

Additional public baths, construction of.

the city of New York is hereby authorized to construct and maintain four free public floating baths in addition to the two now in use in said city, and said additional baths shall be constructed on such plans as the said department shall deem proper, but the work therefor shall be awarded to the lowest bidder with adequate security, as provided by law, and said baths shall be and remain under the exclusive control and management of the said department of public works.

The board of estimate and apportionment to make an appropriation.

§ 2. It shall be the duty of the commissioners of public works to make requisition upon the board of estimate and apportionment within ten days after the passage of an ordinance therefor by the common council of said city for the appropriation of such sum of money, not exceeding sixty thousand dollars, as he may deem necessary for the construction and maintenance of the four additional public floating baths, and it shall be the duty of the board of estimate and apportionment to meet within ten days after the receipt of such requisition and appropriate such sum of money for said purposes.

Comptroller to issue bonds.

§ 3. It shall be the duty of the comptroller of the city of New York, and he is hereby authorized and directed to raise such sums of money as is hereby authorized to be appropriated by the first and second sections of this act, by the issue of revenue bonds, in anticipation of the taxes of the year eighteen hundred and seventy-seven, and said moneys, so to be raised, shall be paid for the construction and maintenance of said baths by the comptroller, on the requisition of the department of. public works. The

Payment of bonds when made.

amount of money necessary to pay said bonds so issued shall be included in the tax levy in the year eighteen hundred and seventy-seven, and the said bonds shall be paid out of the moneys raised by taxation that year.

§ 4. The department of docks of the city of New York shall, upon the requisition of the department of public works of said city, furnish free of charge, in the vicinity of such locations as shall be designated by the department of public works, accessible, convenient, and safe berths for mooring the floating baths herein provided to be constructed and maintained.

Department of docks to provide convenient moorings.

§ 5. This act shall take effect immediately.

Chapter 188.

AN ACT to fix the time for filling in and improving the lands between high and low water mark on the easterly shore of the Harlem river.

Passed April 28, 1876; three-fifths present.

The People of the State of New York, represented in Senate and Assembly, do enact as follows :

SECTION 1. The period of time fixed for the appropriation to the purposes of commerce by the construction of a dock or docks and filling in the same in all letters patent issued by the people of the state of New York to the owners of the adjacent upland, for lands under water and between high and low water mark in front of and adjacent to the lands of the said owners of the adjacent upland on the easterly shore of the Harlem river is hereby extended until two years after the time when plans for the improvement of said river shall be completed by the proper authorities, and copies of such plans filed, one in the office of the register of the city and county of New York, and one in the office of the secretary of state at Albany.

Time extended for improving.

§ 2. Nothing herein contained shall in any way affect any other grants, except those made for the purpose of promoting the commerce of this state, in which a time is limited for the completion of the improvement specified in such letters patent.

§ 3. This act shall take effect immediately.

Chapter 199.

AN ACT in relation to the court of general sessions of the peace in and for the city and county of New York.

Passed May 3, 1876 ; three-fifths present—without the approval of the Governor, pursuant to provision of section nine of article four of the Constitution.

The People of the State of New York, represented in Senate and Assembly, do enact as follows :

Appointment of additional deputy clerks, etc.

SECTION 1. The court of general sessions of the peace of the city and county of New York, is hereby authorized and empowered to appoint two additional deputy clerks, one interpreter, and one stenographer for said court. One of the clerks to be appointed by virtue hereof shall receive an annual salary of twenty-five dundred dollars.

Salary fixed. The stenographer shall receive an annual salary of two thousand dollars ; and one of the clerks and the interpreter, to be appointed by virtue hereof, shall each receive an annual salary of twelve hundred dollars from the date of their appointment.

Provision for payment of salary.

§ 2. The salaries of the clerks, interpreter, and stenographer, whose appointment is hereby authorized, shall be a county charge, and the board of estimate and apportionment of said city and county of New York, shall provide for the payment of the same, so soon as the sums requisite therefor shall be certified to the said board by the said court of general sessions.

§ 3. This act shall take effect immediately.

Chapter 205.

AN ACT in relation to clerks, deputy clerks, and assistant clerks of the several courts of record in the counties of New York and Kings, and of the surrogate's court in said counties.

Passed May 4, 1876.

The People of the State of New York, represented in Senate and Assembly, do enact as follows:

SECTION 1. No clerk, deputy clerk or assistant clerk of any court of record in the counties of New York and Kings, or of the surrogate's court in said counties, shall hereafter be appointed referee, receiver or commissioner under any order or judgment of any court, unless the parties to the action or proceeding mutually agree to such referee. *Not to be appointed referee, receiver, or commissioner.*

§ 2. This act shall take effect immediately.

Chapter 208.

AN ACT to extend the time for making assessments for taxes in the city and county of New York.

Passed May 12, 1876; three-fifths being present.

The People of the State of New York, represented in Senate and Assembly, do enact as follows:

SECTION 1. Any assessments made by the commissioners of taxes and assessments in the city of New York authorized by any law of this state shall be as valid, if made on or before the fourth Monday of March, in the year eighteen hundred and seventy-six, as if they had been made on or before the second Monday in January. *Time for making assessments extended.*

§ 2. This act shall take effect immediately.

Chapter 209.

AN ACT to provide for the completion of the court-house in the third judicial district in the city of New York.

Passed May 12, 1876; three-fifths being present.

The People of the State of New York, represented in Senate and Assembly, do enact as follows:

Comptroller to issue bonds.

SECTION 1. The comptroller of the city of New York is hereby authorized and directed to raise on bonds of said city, for the completion of the court-house for the third judicial district in said city, the sum of fifty thousand dollars, or so much thereof as shall be certified by the commissioners having in charge the erection of said building, to be necessary.

Bonds, when redeemable.

§ 2. The bonds so authorized to be issued, by section one of this act, shall be entitled "Third district court-house bonds of the city of New York," and shall bear interest not exceeding seven per cent., and to be payable in not less than ten nor more than fifty years, as the said comptroller shall determine, and shall not be issued at less than par value. Said bonds shall be signed by the comp-

How signed. troller and countersigned by the mayor, and it shall be the duty of the clerk of the common council to affix the common seal of the corporation thereto and attest the same.

Salaries of commissioners fixed.

§ 3. The board of estimate and apportionment of the city of New York are hereby authorized to fix the salaries or compensation for the services of the three commissioners for the erection of the court-house in the third judicial district of the city of New York, appointed under the provisions of chapter eight hundred and six of the laws of eighteen hundred and seventy-three, from the date of their appointment as such commissioners, and from time to time to make such appropriations therefor as may be necessary;

and it shall be the duty of said commissioners to complete the said court-house building on or before the thirty-first day of December, eighteen hundred and seventy-six, on which date the office of the commissioners for the erection of the court-house in the third judicial district of the city of New York shall be abolished.

Office of commis-' sioner, when abolished.

§ 4. This act shall take effect immediately.

— —

Chapter 210.

AN ACT to repeal chapter nine hundred and twenty of the laws of eighteen hundred and sixty-nine, entitled "An act in relation to the opening, widening, and extending of streets, avenues, and public places in the city of New York."

Passed May 12, 1876; three-fifths being present.

The People of the State of New York, represented in Senate and Assembly, do enact as follows:

SECTION 1. Chapter nine hundred and twenty of the laws of eighteen hundred and sixty-nine, entitled "An act in relation to the opening, widening, and extending of streets, avenues, and public places in the city of New York," is hereby repealed. Provided, however, that no existing right or interest lawfully created or established by and under the provisions of said act, and no action or proceeding now pending, lawfully commenced and prosecuted, shall be affected or in any manner prejudiced or invalidated by the repeal thereof.

§ 2. This act shall take effect immediately.

Chapter 211.

AN ACT for the relief of the creditors of James B. Taylor, late of the city of New York, deceased.

Passed May 12, 1876.

The People of the State of New York, represented in Senate and Assembly, do enact as follows:

SECTION 1. Upon the petition of any judgment creditor of the estate of James B. Taylor, late of the city of New York, deceased, whose judgment shall have been recovered since the decease of said James B. Taylor, the surrogate of the county of New York shall have power to appoint some suitable person as receiver of the real estate left by the said James B. Taylor, pending the contest upon his last will and testament. Such receiver shall have and possess the same power and authority, and shall be required to give the same security as if appointed by any other court of competent jurisdiction. The said surrogate shall have the same power to remove such receiver and appoint another in his stead as is possessed by the supreme court in cases of receivers appointed by it, and may in like manner direct and control his conduct from time to time.

Surrogate to appoint receiver.

§ 2. Whenever it shall be made to appear to said surrogate by the petition of the said receiver, or of any such judgment creditor or creditors of the said James B. Taylor, that the personal estate of the said James B. Taylor is insufficient to pay all the debts of the said Taylor, together with the cost and expenses of administration, the said surrogate of the county of New York shall have power and authority to order the real estate of the said James B. Taylor, or any part of the same, to be leased, mortgaged or sold by the said receiver in the same manner as if applied for by an executor or administrator, as now pro-

Real estate to be sold or leased, etc.

vided by law; to direct such receiver to execute and deliver any lease, mortgage or conveyance necessary to carry into effect such order of the said surrogate, and to require the money arising from such lease, mortgage or sale, after paying the costs and expenses of the same, to be brought into said surrogate's court, to be distributed, paid out and applied as required by law in case of a lease, mortgage or sale made by an executor or administrator under the order of a surrogate, as now authorized and provided by law.

§ 3. The said petition shall set forth: first, the amount, character and value of the personal property of said deceased, remaining; second, the debts outstanding against the said James B. Taylor; third, a general description of all the real estate of which the said James B. Taylor died seized, situated in this State, with the estimated value of the same and the incumbrances, if any thereon (designating such parts as have been sold for taxes or in foreclosure), and whether occupied or not, and if occupied the name of the occupant or occupants; fourth, the names, ages, and residence of the heirs-at-law of said James B. Taylor, and also of the devisees named in his alleged will; and all the matters required to be stated in such petition shall be stated as fully and particularly as the same can be ascertained, and such petition shall be verified by the petitioner or his attorney, to the effect that the same is true to the knowledge of the deponent, except as to the matters therein stated on his information and belief, and that as to those matters he believes it to be true. If the affidavit be by an attorney, the reason why the petitioner does not make the same shall be stated. If there be more than one petitioner, the verification may be by any one of those jointly interested. _{Petition, what it shall set forth.}

§ 4. Upon presenting such petition to the surrogate of the county of New York, said surrogate shall proceed in the same manner as upon the petition of an executor or administrator applying to the surrogate for authority to mortgage, lease, or sell so much of the real estate of the testator or intestate as shall be necessary to pay his debts, and shall in like manner determine whether such real estate shall be leased, mortgaged or sold; and the order of the said surrogate in the premises shall be executed by the said receiver, as in the case of an order for an executor or an administrator to lease, mortgage, or sell the real estate of his testator or intestate, and the moneys produced by such lease, mortgage or sale shall be brought into the office of said surrogate, as in such case; and the said surrogate shall apply and distribute such moneys among the creditors of the said James B. Taylor, and in all respects proceed as he is required by law to do on a similar application by an executor or administrator.

Proceeds of sales, etc., to be distributed among creditors.

§ 5. Upon receiving the petition above mentioned, the jurisdiction of the said surrogate shall continue, and the said surrogate shall proceed until the creditors of said James B. Taylor are paid in full, or so far as the proceeds of the said real estate will pay the said debts.

Surplus to be deposited or invested.

§ 6. If, after the payment of said debts and the said costs and expenses, there shall be any surplus of the proceeds of the sale, the same shall be deposited or invested by said surrogate in his name of office to abide the determination of such contest upon said will, and when such contest is finally determined, such surplus or any surplus which may arise shall be paid over to the parties entitled thereto.

§ 7. Any order or decree made by the surrogate under the provisions of this act may be reviewed on appeal to the supreme court within thirty days after such order or decree shall have been made, and such court may thereupon affirm, reverse, or modify the same.

§ 8. This act shall take effect immediately.

Chapter 212.

AN ACT to make further provision for the audit and payment of the claims and expenses of conducting civil and criminal suits and proceedings growing out of the frauds upon the treasury of the city and county of New York.

Passed May 12, 1876 ; three-fifths being present.

The People of the State of New York, represented in Senate and Assembly, do enact as follows:

SECTION 1. The board of supervisors of the county of New York is hereby authorized and required to raise by tax upon the estates, real and personal, in the city and county of New York subject to taxation, in the year one thousand eight hundred and seventy-six, twenty-five thousand dollars, for the purposes hereinafter mentioned. *Board of supervisors to raise by tax.*

§ 2. The said sum of twenty-five thousand dollars, in addition to sums heretofore appropriated by chapter five hundred and eight of the laws of eighteen hundred and seventy-two, and chapter six hundred and thirty-one of the laws of eighteen hundred and seventy-three, and chapter three hundred and fifty-nine of the laws of eighteen hundred and seventy-four, shall be applied to the payment of the liabilities and expenses for counsel fees, and otherwise, which have been or may be incurred by the attorney-general and Charles O'Conor, or under their direction, or that of either of them, in the conduct and prosecution of suits and criminal proceedings connected with or growing out of the alleged frauds mentioned in said act, chapter five hundred and eight of the laws of eighteen hundred and seventy-two ; said liabilities shall be paid by the comptroller of the city of New York, on production of accounts therefor duly certified by the attorney-general and the governor. *Payment of expenses and counsel fees.*

§ 3. This act shall take effect immediately

Chapter 213.

AN ACT to amend chapter one hundred and six of the laws of eighteen hundred and sixty-five, entitled "An act to incorporate the New York Infant Asylum."

Passed May 13, 1876; three-fifths being present.

The People of the State of New York, represented in Senate and Assembly, do enact as follows:

Incorporation of.

SECTION 1. Section twenty-two of chapter one hundred and six of the laws of eighteen hundred and sixty-five, entitled "An act to incorporate the New York Infant Asylum," as amended by chapter two hundred and sixty-three of the laws of eighteen hundred and seventy-two, entitled an act to amend an act entitled an act to incorporate the New York Infant Asylum, passed March eleventh, eighteen hundred and sixty-five, is hereby further amended so as to read as follows:

Board of supervisors to raise by tax.

§ 22. In each and every year after this act shall take effect, the board of supervisors of the city and county of New York shall levy and collect by tax at the same time and in the same manner as the contingent charges and expenses of the city and county are levied and collected, and pay over to said corporation such a sum per week for every infant under eighteen months of age, for whose care some provision has not been made by some person or persons as the commissioners of charities and corrections shall certify to have been expended during the last fiscal year, in the care and provision for the infants per week each, in the infants' hospital, which is under the control of said commissioners; and for every child over the age of eighteen months such a sum per year, in monthly payments,

Maintenance and care of each child.

as the said commissioners shall certify to have been ex-

pended as an average cost for maintenance and the
hospital care of each child, for a full year, at the institution known as the Nursery for Children on Randall's Island,
in the last previous fiscal year, as shown and reported by
said commissioners, and the said commissioners shall so
inform and certify, upon the request of the managers of
said asylum, on or before the fifteenth day of February,
in each year, and such certification shall be based upon the
total expenditures charged and chargeable by the said commissioners against their said infants' hospital and their
said nursery (according to the ages of the children continuing in the house), and proportionately for any fraction
of a year for each any every child which agreeable to the
provisions of this act, shall be entrusted to the care and
custody of the said corporation from the city and county
of New York, and shall be supported and maintained by Care and
them. It is further provided that whenever any homeless attendance
or needy mother has received care and attendance in the
lying in wards of the New York Infant Asylum, the managers of said asylum shall be entitled to receive, and shall
receive, from the county treasurer, as hereinabove provided, the sum of twenty-five dollars for said care and
obstetric attendance, and whenever any mother thus
domiciled and attended at the birth of her child, and
whenever any other homeless or needy mother with a
nursing infant, resides at the asylum by the request of its
officers, and wetnurses her own infant, the managers of
said institution shall be entitled to receive and shall receive
from the county treasurer, the sum of eighteen dollars per
month, and proportionately for any fraction of a month
for each mother so remaining under their charge in said
asylum, provided such residence shall exceed the period
of two months, to be paid as hereinbefore provided in
monthly, quarterly or annual payments, as said managers
may request, but the managers of the said institution shall
not be entitled to receive the said monthly allowance for

a longer period than for one year for any mother so remaining.

§ 2. This act shall take effect immediately.

Chapter 274.

AN ACT in relation to arrears of taxes in the city of New York, and to provide for the reissuing of revenue bonds in anticipation of such taxes.

Passed May 15, 1876; three-fifths present.

The People of the State of New York, represented in Senate and Assembly, do enact as follows:

SECTION 1. At any time within one year after the passage of this act, any person may pay to the comptroller of the city of New York, the amount of any tax upon property, real or personal, belonging to such person, heretofore laid or imposed and now remaining unpaid, together with interest at seven per cent. per annum, to be calculated from the time that such tax was imposed to the time of such payment, and the comptroller shall make and deliver to the person so making such payment a receipt therefor, and shall forthwith cancel the record of any such tax. Upon such payment such tax shall cease to be a lien upon the property and shall be deemed fully paid, satisfied, and discharged, and there shall be no right to any further interest or penalty by reason of such tax not having been paid within the time heretofore required by law, or by reason of any statute heretofore passed requiring the payment of any penalty or interest over seven per cent. upon any unpaid tax.

§ 2. Any revenue bonds heretofore issued in anticipation of the taxes in the first section specified which may

Arrears of taxes, how and when paid.

Tax ceasing to be a lien.

Reissue of revenue bonds.

fall due and become payable before such taxes are collected, may be reissued by the comptroller of said city, in whole or in part, for such period as he may determine, not exceeding one year.

§ 3. This act shall take effect immediately.

Chapter 275.

AN ACT for the relief of Cornelius Flynn.

Passed May 15, 1876; three-fifths being present.

The People of the State of New York, represented in Senate and Assembly, do enact as follows :

SECTION 1. The comptroller of the city of New York is hereby authorized and required to examine into the claim of Cornelius Flynn for services rendered by him as acting assistant clerk of the district court in the city of New York for the first judicial district, during the months of January, February, March, April, May, and June, in the year eighteen hundred and seventy-five; and upon the production to said comptroller of the original certificate of appointment of said Cornelius Flynn to the office of assistant clerk of said district court by the justice holding office as justice of said district court at the time of the execution of such certificate, a certified copy of the official bond executed by said Cornelius Flynn, and certificate of the filing thereof with the county clerk of the city and county of New York, and the certificate by said justice so holding office as justice of said district court during the period of said alleged services of the performance by said Cornelius Flynn of the duties of said office during said period, accompanied by the affidavit of said Flynn, verifying the truth of such certificate, the said comptroller shall audit and certify the amount of such claim at the rate established by

Comptroller to examine claim.

law as the compensation for the services of the clerks of the said district courts in the city of New York at the time of the rendition of such services, and report the same to the board of estimate and apportionment of said city, who shall thereupon make an appropriation for the payment of the amount thereof, for which amount the said comptroller shall thereupon draw his warrant upon the treasury of the city of New York, and deliver the same to said Cornelius Flynn in satisfaction of said claim ; and it is further provided that the comptroller of the city of New York shall be authorized and directed to issue and sell bonds of the city of New York to raise the amount necessary to pay such amount in full with interest, which shall be levied and assessed on the taxable property of the city and county of New York.

Board of estimate and apportionment to provide for payment of claim when audited.

Chapter 291.

AN ACT making an appropriation to the commissioners of emigration to enable them to perform the duties imposed upon them by law.

Passed May 15, 1876, by a two-third vote.

The People of the State of New York, represented in Senate and Assembly, do enact as follows:

SECTION 1. The comptroller of the state is hereby authorized and directed to draw his several warrants upon the treasurer, who shall pay the same respectively when presented, in favor of the commissioners of emigration, for such amounts as they may, from time to time, require for the purpose of paying the current expenses, during the year commencing on the first day of May, eighteen hundred and seventy-six, which warrants shall not exceed in the aggregate the sum of two hundred thousand dollars,

Comptroller of the state to provide for the payment of expenses of commission.

Amount limited.

but whenever any appropriation shall be made by the Congress of the United States for the purposes herein mentioned, no more money shall be paid under this act.

§ 2. The said sum of two hundred thousand dollars, or so much thereof as may be necessary, is hereby appropriated for the payment of the warrants in and by the first section of this act mentioned and authorized which shall be paid out of any moneys in the treasury not otherwise appropriated.

§ 3. The comptroller is hereby prohibited, however, from drawing his warrant upon the state treasurer in favor of the commissioners of emigration, against the funds hereby appropriated, unless a detailed account of their expenses, for which a warrant is desired, be at such time presented to the comptroller, duly verified by said commissioners or a majority of them, and such warrant shall in no case exceed in amount the expenses incurred by such commissioners, and for which such detailed account is presented as aforesaid.

Detailed account of expenses must be furnished.

§ 4. This act shall take effect immediately.

Chapter 296.

AN ACT to provide for the determination and payment of the amount due by the city of New York to that portion of the town of Westchester, which, prior to January one, eighteen hundred and seventy-four, was part of joint union school district number two, of the town of West Farms, for school property taken by the city of New York.

Passed May 15, 1876; three-fifths being present.

The People of the State of New York, represented in Senate and Assembly, do enact as follows:

SECTION 1. The board of education of the city of New York, and the board of education of school district number four of the town of Westchester, in the county of Westchester, shall examine, audit, and determine the amount which ought, proportionally and fairly, to be paid by the mayor, aldermen, and commonalty of the city of New York to the inhabitants and estates of that portion of the town of Westchester, which, prior to the annexation of the town of West Farms to the city of New York, formed part of the joint union school district, number two, of the town of West Farms, for their contribution by payment of taxes, to the cost of the land, schoolhouse, furniture, books, apparatus, and other school property, which, by such annexation, was vested in and declared to be the property of the mayor, aldermen, and commonalty of the city of New York, and for their interest in the same, and their loss sustained by the vesting thereof in said city of New York. The amount found due on said audit, examination, and determination, with interest thereon from the first day of January, eighteen hundred and seventy-four, shall be paid by the mayor, aldermen, and commonalty of the city of New York, to the board of education of school district number four, of the town of Westchester, whose duty it is hereby made to receive the same for the benefit of said inhabitants and estates of said portion of the town of Westchester. In case of failure of said boards to agree upon the amount so to be paid, within six months after the passage of this act, the supreme court, in the second department, shall have power and jurisdiction to determine such amount, after hearing, in an action which said board of education of school district number four, of the town of Westchester, is hereby authorized to commence, after six months, and within one year, from the passage of this act, in the name of said board, against the mayor, aldermen, and commonalty of the city of New York, and in said action said court shall adjudge the payment of such amount as shall proportionally and fairly be due upon the principles hereinbefore declared.

Proportion of tax to be paid to the county of Westchester.

Failure of both boards to agree.

§ 2. Within ninety days after the passage of this act the comptroller of the city of New York is hereby directed to borrow, on the credit of the mayor, aldermen and commonalty of the city of New York, on bonds of the said city, to be denominated revenue bonds, and in anticipation of the collection of the taxes to be levied and imposed on the property, real and personal, subject to taxation in the city and county of New York for the year one thousand eight hundred and seventy-six, the sum of ten thousand dollars for the purpose of paying the amount which shall be audited and determined to be due as aforesaid. The revenue bonds herein mentioned shall bear interest at the rate of not exceeding seven per cent. per annum. *Comptroller to issue bonds.*

§ 3. It shall be the duty of the said comptroller of the city of New York, and he is hereby directed to pay, within ten days after the determination of the amount due as aforesaid, the money derived from the sale of said bonds to the said board of education of school district number four, of the town of Westchester, so far as the same may be necessary to pay the amount so determined or adjudged to be due, with interest to the day of payment. *Comptroller to pay with interest.*

§ 4. The board of estimate and apportionment of New York are hereby authorized, directed and required to cause to be included in the taxes to be levied and raised in the said city of New York for the year one thousand eight hundred and seventy-six, upon the estates subject to taxation in the city and county of New York, an amount sufficient to pay the revenue bonds herein directed to be issued by the said comptroller in anticipation of the collection of the said taxes, with all interest due or to become due thereon. *Amount thus paid to be raised by taxes.*

§ 5. For the purpose of this act, all acts or parts of acts inconsistent with this act are hereby repealed.

§ 6. This act shall take effect immediately.

Chapter 300.

AN ACT for the relief of Patrick McCabe.

Passed May 15, 1876; three-fifths being present.

The People of the State of New York, represented in Senate and Assembly, do enact as follows:

Comptroller to examine claim.

SECTION 1. The comptroller of the city of New York is hereby authorized and required to examine into the claim of Patrick McCabe, for services rendered by him as acting assistant clerk of the district court in the city of New York, for the third judicial district, from the first day of January, eighteen hundred and seventy-four, to the first day of July, eighteen hundred and seventy-five; and upon the production to said comptroller of the original certificate of appointment of said Patrick McCabe to the office of assistant clerk of said district court, by the justice holding office as justice of said district court at the time of the execution of such certificate, a certified copy of the official bond executed by said Patrick McCabe, and a certificate of the filing thereof with the county clerk of the city and county of New York, and the certificate of the justice holding office as justice of said district court during the period of said alleged services, of the performance by said Patrick McCabe of the duties of said office during said period, accompanied by the affidavit of said McCabe verifying the truth of such certificate, the comptroller shall audit and certify the amount of such claim at the rate established by law as the compensation for the services of the clerks of the said district courts in the city of New York at the time of the rendition of such services,

Board of apportionment to provide for payment of claim, when audited.

and report the same to the board of estimate and apportionment of said city, who shall thereupon make an appropriation for the payment of the amount thereof, for which amount the said comptroller shall thereupon draw his warrant upon the treasury of the city of New York, and deliver the same to said Patrick McCabe, in satisfaction of said claim; and it is further provided that the comptroller of the city of New York shall be authorized and directed to issue and sell bonds of the city of New York to raise the amount necessary to pay such amount in full with interest, which shall be levied and assessed on the taxable property of the city and county of New York.

Chapter 316.

AN ACT relative to judgments entered upon forfeited recognizances in the city and county of New York.

Passed May 15, 1876.

The People of the State of New York, represented in Senate and Assembly, do enact as follows:

SECTION 1. The court of common pleas for the city and county of New York, upon the certificate of the district attorney of the county of New York, that the people of the state of New York have lost no rights by reason of the failure of a surety to produce a principal in compliance with the terms of a recognizance given by them, and that by reason of the principal being produced, the said people of the state of New York are in as good a position to prosecute said principal as when such failure occurred, may by order vacate and set aside any judgment heretofore entered, or that may be hereafter entered, upon the forfeiture of such recognizance against such principal or surety, or either of them, on payment to the chamberlain of the city of New York of all costs included in such judgment and of all expenses incurred in the apprehension or recapture of such principal.

§ 2. This act shall take effect immediately.

Chapter 356.

AN ACT in relation to summary proceedings in the city of New York, to recover the possession of lands for non-payment of rent and for holding over after expiration of term.

Passed May 19, 1876; three-fifths being present.

The People of the State of New York, represented in Senate and Assembly, do enact as follows:

Dispossess proceedings. where returnable.

SECTION 1. No proceedings shall be taken before any justice of any district court of the city of New York to dispossess any tenant or tenants under the statute in relation to summary proceedings to recover the possession of lands unless the summons is returnable and all the proceedings are before such justice at the district court-house, or the building designated by the mayor, aldermen and commonalty of the city of New York as the place where the court of said justice shall be held.

Clerk to pay to the comptroller all costs and fees.

§ 2. All costs and fees allowed by law to any such justice in any such proceeding shall be paid to the clerk of the district court of the justice before whom such proceeding is commenced, and every such clerk shall, monthly, on the last day of each month, account for, return and pay over all such costs and fees therefor paid to the comptroller of the city of New York.

§ 3. This act shall take effect immediately.

Chapter 372.

AN ACT to amend chapter four hundred and twenty-one
of the laws of eighteen hundred and seventy-four,
entitled "An act to secure to children the benefits of
an elementary education."

Passed May 20, 1876; three-fifths being present.

*The People of the State of New York, represented in
Senate and Assembly, do hereby enact as follows:*

SECTION 1. Section two of chapter four hundred and
twenty-one of the laws of eighteen hundred and seventy-
four, entitled "An act to secure to children the benefits of
an elementary education," is hereby amended so as to read
as follows:

§ 2. No child under the age of fourteen years shall be
employed by any person to labor in any business whatever
during the school hours of any school day of the school
term of the public school in the school district of the city
where such child is, unless such child shall have attended
some public or private day school where instruction was
given by a teacher qualified to instruct in spelling, reading,
writing, geography, English grammar and arithmetic, or
shall have been regularly instructed at home in said
branches, by some person qualified to instruct in the same,
at least fourteen weeks of the fifty-two weeks next preceding any and every year in which such child shall be
employed, and shall, at the time of such employment, deliver to the employer a certificate in writing, signed by the
teacher or school trustee of the district, or of a school, and
countersigned by such officer as the board of education or
public instruction, by whatever name it may be known in
any city, incorporated village or town, shall designate,
certifying to such attendance or instruction, and any person who shall employ any child contrary to the provisions

*Children un-
der fourteen
not to be
employed
during
school hours.*

*Those re-
ceiving in-
struction
excepted.*

*Certificate of
instruction
to be de-
livered to
employers.*

of this section, shall for each offense forfeit and pay a
penalty of fifty dollars to the treasurer or chief fiscal officer
of the city or supervisor of the town in which such offense
shall occur; the said sum or penalty, when so paid, to be
added to the public shool money of the school district in
which the offense occurred.

§ 2. Section three of said act is herby amended so as to
read as follows :

§ 3. It shall be the duty of the trustee or trustees of
every school district, or public school, or union school, or
of officers appointed for that purpose by the board of education or public instruction, by whatever name it may be
known, in every town or city, in the months of September
and of February of each year, and at such times as may be
deemed necessary, to examine into the situation of the
children employed in all manufacturing and other estab-
lishments in such school districts where children are employed, and in case any town or city is not divided into
school districts, it shall, for the purposes of the examination provided for in this section, be divided by the school
authorities thereof into districts, and the said trustees or
other officers as aforesaid, notified of their respective districts on or before the first day of January of each year,
and the said trustee or trustees, or other officers as aforesaid, shall ascertain whether all of the provisions of this
act are duly observed, and report all violations thereof to
the treasurer or chief fiscal officer of said city or supervisor

of said town. On such examination the proprietor, superintendent, or manager of said establishment shall, on
demand, exhibit to said examining trustee or other officers
as aforesaid, a correct list of all children between the ages
of eight and fourteen years, employed in said establishment, with said certificates of attendance on school or of
instruction.

§ 3. Section 5 of said act is hereby amended so as to read as follows :

§ 5. The trustee or trustees of any school district or public school, or the president of any union school, or such officer as the board of education of said city, incorporated village or town may designate, is hereby authorized and empowered to see that sections one, two, three, four, and five of this act are enforced, and to report in writing all violations thereof to the treasurer or chief fiscal officer of this city, or to the supervisor of his town ; any person who shall violate any provision of sections one, three, and four of this act shall, on written notice of such violation from one of the school officers above named, forfeit for the first offense, any pay to the treasurer or chief fiscal officer of the city, or to the supervisor of the town in which he resides, or such offense has occurred, the sum of one dollar, and after such first offense, shall for each succeeding offense in the same year, forfeit and pay to the treasurer of said city, or supervisor of said town, the sum of five dollars for each and every week, not exceeding thirteen weeks in any one year, during which he, after written notice from said school officer, shall have failed to comply with any of said provisions ; the said penalties, when paid, to be added to the public school money of said school district in which the offense occured. *School officers must report violations.* *Penalty for the first offense.* *For succeeding offenses.*

§ 4. Section seven of said act is hereby amended so as to read as follows :

§ 7. In case any person having the control of any child between the ages of eight and fourteen years is unable to induce said child to attend school for the said fourteen weeks in each year, and shall so state in writing to said trustee or said other officers, appointed by the board of education or public instruction, by whatever name it may be known, the said child shall, from and after the date and delivery to said trustee or other officer as aforesaid of said

Habitual
truant, how
dealt with.

statement in writing, be deemed and dealt with as an habitual truant, and said person shall be relieved of all penalties incurred for said year after said date, under sections one, four, and five of this act, as to such child.

§ 5. Section eight of said act is hereby amended so as to read as follows:

Board of
education
empowered
to make pro-
vision con-
cerning
habitual
truants.

§ 8. The board of education or public instruction, by whatever name it may be called, in such city and incorporated village, and the trustees of the school districts and union schools in each town, by an affirmative vote of a majority of said trustees, at a meeting or meetings to be called for this purpose, on ten days' notice, in writing to each trustee, said notice to be given by the town clerk, are for each of their respective cities and towns hereby authorized and empowered and directed, on or before the first day of January, 1877, to make all needful provisions, arrangements, rules and regulations concerning habitual truants, and children between said ages of eight and four-

Children
found
wandering
during
school
hours.

teen years of age, who may be found wandering about the streets or public places of said city or town during school hours of the school day of the term of the public school of said city or town, having no lawful occupation or business, and growing up in ignorance; and said provisions, arrangements, rules and regulations shall be such as shall, in their judgment, be most conducive to the welfare of such children, and to the good order of said city or town: and

Places of
discipline
and instruc-
tion.

shall provide suitable places for the discipline and instruction and confinement, when necessary, of such children, and may require the aid of the police of cities or incorporated villages and constables of towns to enforce their said rules and regulations; provided, however, that such provisions, arrangements, rules and regulations, shall not go into effect as laws for said several cities and towns until they shall have been approved in writing by a justice of the Supreme Court, for the judicial district in which said city, incorporated village or town is situated, and when so approved he shall file the same with the clerk of the said city, incorporated village or town, who shall print the same and furnish ten copies thereof to each trustee of each school district, or public or union school of said city, incorporated village or town; the said trustees shall keep one copy thereof posted in a conspicuous place, in or upon each school house in his charge during the school terms each year. In like manner the same in each city, incorporated village or town may be amended or revised within six months after the passage of this act, and thereafter annually as the trustee or trustees of any school district, or public school, or the president of any union school, or the board of education or public instruction, or by whatever name it may be known, in any city, incorporated village or town, may determine.

Rules and regulations to be approved of by a justice of the supreme court.

Copies of rules to be posted in each school house.

Rules may be amended.

§ 6. This act shall take effect immediately.

Chapter 376.

AN ACT to prevent the deposit of mud, earth, soil, ashes, or refuse in the North or Hudson river, and to prevent the filling up the navigable waters of said river, and to preserve the navigation thereof.

Passed May 20, 1876; three-fifths being present.

The People of the State of New York, represented in Senate and Assembly, do enact as follows:

SECTION 1. It shall be unlawful for any person or persons, by means of any boats, scows, or vessels, or in any other manner whatever, to cast, throw, dump, or deposit any mud, earth, soil, ashes, refuse, stone, rock, or other solid substance or materials, into the waters of the North or Hudson river, or to place, construct, or build any con-

No refuse to be dumped.

or obstruction placed in the river.

trivance, substance, or thing whatever, within said waters, which shall or may operate in any manner whatever to lessen or decrease the depth of such waters, or in any manner whatever interfere with navigation therein, or imperil or jeopardize the free and safe navigation thereof, or tend in any manner thereto; provided, however, that **Exceptions.** nothing herein shall prevent any steamboat or steam vessel from dumping or casting into said river at any point not between the city of New York and Stoney Point, or between Tivoli and the State dam above Troy, any ashes which shall be accumulated upon such boat or vessel upon any trip.

Penalties. § 2. Any person designedly doing any act forbidden by the provisions of this act shall be deemed guilty of a misdemeanor and liable to imprisonment for a term of not more than sixty days, or to a fine of not more than one hundred dollars, or both, in the discretion of the court, for each and every offense, and may be arrested by the authorities of either of the counties adjacent to the Hudson river at the location where such offense shall be committed. The courts in said counties, respectively, shall have concurrent power and jurisdiction to try such offender or offenders, whether the offense be committed in the respective county or not. Any constable, policeman, sheriff, under or deputy sheriff, alderman of a city or trustee of a village, in either of said counties, finding or **Offenders can be arrested without warrant.** seeing any person or persons offending against the provisions of this act, may and it is hereby declared to be his duty to arrest, without warrant, such person or persons so offending, and them to take before the nearest magistrate to be dealt with for such offense according to law.

Additional penalties. § 3. Any persons offending against the provisions of this act, shall also forfeit and pay a penalty of fifty dollars for each offense, to be recovered by suit or action at law in any court having jurisdiction. Such action may be

brought in any county adjacent to said river, in the name
of any municipal corporation, or in the name of any commissioner of highways or overseers of the poor of any
town located within either of said counties, and the sum
of money recovered in such action shall be for the super- Fines to be used for benefit of the poor.
visors of the county in which such action is tried, for the
benefit of the poor of said county.

§ 4. This act shall not apply to the depositing of sub- Act not to apply in certain cases.
stances upon the building of wharves or piers upon, or the
filling in of land under water granted by the people of the
state of New York to any person, or the waters now dyked
off by the river commissioners for improving the channel
of the river, or when such act, which otherwise would be
an offense, is done by the owner of such land or under his
authority, or by his direction or by direction of any public
officer having charge of the improvement of the river.
Nor shall this act apply to the sweeping, washing, or clear-
ing from the decks of canal boats, freight, passenger or
pleasure boats or vessels, of such dirt only as collects
naturally thereon from the use thereof of human beings
using the same for transportation or pleasure, nor the haul-
ing of fire from the furnance-grate, of any steamboat having state rooms above the main deck, provided no coal or
ashes shall be dumped from the ash-box of said steamboat
except as authorized in the first section of this act, nor to the
setting of shad poles in the shad season ; nor to the use of Shad poles, etc., allowed to be set in the season within certain limits.
any other devices or contrivances for the purposes of fish-
ing in any season of the year, but no such setting of shad
poles or devices for fishing shall be allowed below the
northerly line established by the harbor commissioners of
the city of New York ; nor shall this act apply to throwing overboard the refuse and waste matter which ordina-
rily accumulates in and about canal boats engaged in the
transportation of goods and merchandise. But this act
shall not be construed to authorize the throwing in said
water of food or any contrivance or device in which food
may be kept, carried, or preserved.

§ 5. In case the mud-scow from which such mud, earth, soil, ashes, refuse, stone, rock, or other solid substance shall be cast, thrown, dumped, or deposited, as specified in section 1, shall be towed by a steamboat or tug to the point at which such substance shall be thrown, dropped, *Masters of vessels and contractors to be jointly liable for violations.* cast, dumped, or deposited, the master of such steamboat or tug and the contractor using the same shall be jointly and severally liable to a penalty of two hundred dollars for each and every such offense, recoverable in an action by any overseer of the poor, or supervisor of any town located within any of said counties, in any court having jurisdiction of an action for penalties, not exceeding two hundred dollars, for the supervisors of the county in which such action is tried for the benefit of the poor of said county.

Penalties for compromising for violations. § 6. Any person who shall accept any money or other valuable thing by way of compromise for the violation of any of the provisions of this act, without the approval of the court, shall be deemed guilty of a misdemeanor.

Chapter 409.

AN ACT to enable the court of general sessions of the peace of the city and county of New York to appoint an interpreter.

Passed May 24, 1876 ; three-fifths being present.

The People of the State of New York, represented in Senate and Assembly, do enact as follows :

Appointment of, and salary fixed. SECTION 1. The court of general sessions of the peace is hereby authorized and empowered to appoint an interpreter for said court. The interpreter to be appointed by virtue hereof shall receive an annual compensation, to be fixed by said court, not to exceed two thousand five hundred dollars per annum.

§ 2. The expense of carrying into execution the provisions of this act and the salary of the said interpreter whose appointment is hereby authorized, shall be a county charge, and the board of estimate and apportionment of said city and county of New York shall provide for the payment of the same, so soon as the sums requisite therefor shall be certified to the said board by the said court of general sessions.

Board of estimate and apportionment to provide for the payment of salary.

§ 3. This act shall take effect immediately. .

Chapter 411.

AN ACT to amend chapter three hundred and twenty-nine of the Laws of eighteen hundred and seventy-four, entitled "An act to re-enact and amend an act, entitled 'An act to provide for the annexation of the towns of Morrisania, West Farms, and Kingsbridge, in the county of Westchester, to the city and county of New York,'" passed May twenty-three, eighteen hundred and seventy-three.

Passed May 25, 1876 ; three-fifths being present.

The People of the State of New York, represented in Senate and Assembly, do enact as follows :

SECTION 1. Section seventeen of chapter three hundred and twenty-nine of the laws of eighteen hundred and seventy-four, entitled "An act to re-enact and amend an act to provide for the annexation of the towns of Morrisania, West Farms, and Kingsbridge, in the county of Westchester, to the city and county of New York," passed May twenty-third, eighteen hundred and seventy-three, is hereby amended to read as follows :

§ 17. (1.) It shall be the duty of the board of commissioners of the department of public parks of the city of

New York to cause to be made maps of the territory constituting the twenty-third and twenty-fourth wards, as defined by this act, for the use of the department of taxes and assessments of New York city. Such maps shall show all street, road, and property lines, and the divisions of all lots and separate properties, and the dimensions of the same. The said maps shall be of such scale, form, and dimensions, and bound in volumes of such size as may be directed by the commissioners of taxes and assessments. The said lots and separate property shall be designated on said maps by numbers, as may be directed by the Commissioners of taxes and assessments.

(2.) The commissioners of the department of public parks shall cause such maps and such surveys as may be found necessary for their completion, to be made by competent surveyors and draughtsmen in the office and under the direction of the civil and topographical engineer in charge of surveying, laying out, and monumenting the twenty-third and twenty-fourth wards, and, so far as practicable, from the maps of topographical surveys of the town of Morrisania, made under the direction of the commissioners appointed under chapter eight hundred and forty-one of the laws of eighteen hundred and sixty-eight, and the topographical maps of the towns of West Farms and Kingsbridge, made under the direction of the commissioners of the Central park and the commissioners of the department of public parks, which said maps are now in the possession of said department of public parks.

(3.) The board of estimate and apportionment of the city of New York is hereby authorized to appropriate from any unexpended balances for the year eighteen hundred and seventy-five the sum of ten thousand dollars, for the use of the department of public parks, to pay for work which may be done under this act during the year eighteen hundred and seventy-six.

(4.) The board of estimate and apportionment of the city of New York shall annually include in the estimate of the amounts necessary to pay the expenses of conducting the business of the department of public parks of the city of New York such sum or sums of money as shall in the judgment and discretion of said board be necessary to carry on the work authorized by this act.

§ 2. This act shall take effect immediately.

Chapter 413.

AN ACT in relation to the clerks, officers, and attendants of the marine court of the city of New York.

Passed May 25, 1876; three-fifths present.

The People of the State of New York, represented in Senate and Assembly, do enact as follows:

SECTION 1. The marine court of the city of New York shall hereafter be entitled to the following number of clerks, assistant clerks, stenographers, attendants, and interpreters: one clerk, three deputy clerks; not more than ten assistant clerks; not more than three stenographers; not more than thirteen attendants, and one interpreter.

Number of clerks, attendants, etc., designated.

§ 2. The said clerks, officers, attendants, and interpreter of said court shall receive the following salaries: The clerk, four thousand dollars; one deputy clerk, three thousand five hundred dollars; and the other deputy clerks three thousand dollars each; the assistant clerks, two thousand dollars each; the stenographers, two thousand dollars each; the attendants, twelve hundred dollars each, and the interpreter, fifteen hundred dollars.

Salaries of, fixed.

§ 3. The chief clerk of said marine court may be removed by the court at pleasure, and any vacancy by removal or otherwise shall be filled by the court.

Chief clerk, how removed.

§ 4. The several deputy clerks, assistant clerks, stenographers, attendants, and interpreter may be removed by the chief clerk of said court at pleasure, and any vacancy by removal or otherwise shall be filled by the said clerk.

Deputy clerks, etc., removal of.

§ 5. The provisions of any act inconsistent with the provisions of this act, are hereby repealed.

§ 6. This act shall take effect immediately.

Chapter 414.

AN ACT to amend chapter six hundred and seventy-one of the laws of eighteen hundred and fifty-seven, entitled "An act to establish regulations for the port of New York."

Passed May 25, 1876 ; three-fifths present.

The People of the State of New York, represented in Senate and Assembly, do enact as follows:

SECTION 1. Section seven of chapter six hundred and seventy-one of the laws of eighteen hundred and fifty-seven, entitled "An act to establish regulations for the port of New York," is hereby amended so as to read as follows:

§ 7. When any slip, basin, or shoal in the port of New York shall be dredged or excavated, it shall be the duty of the person or persons causing the same to be dredged to cause the sand, mud, or other material so dredged to be towed to sea to a point at least three miles outside of Sandy Hook, or deposited at some place above

Mud, sand, etc., how disposed of.

high-water mark, or to be deposited behind a bulkhead for filling; and any person wilfully violating the provisions of this section shall forfeit and pay to the said commissioners the sum of five dollars for every cubic yard removed not so disposed of, one-half of which shall be retained by the commissioners.

§ 2. This act shall take effect immediately.

Chapter 429.

AN ACT to provide for payment for the use and occupation of armories and drill-rooms in the city of New York.

Passed May 26, 1876; three-fiths being present.

The People of the State of New York, represented in Senate and Assembly, do enact as follows:

SECTION 1. Whenever any building or buildings in the city of New York, between the first day of January, eighteen hundred and seventy-one, and the first day of May, eighteen hundred and seventy-six, has or have been, or shall be, in whole or in part, actually used and occupied as an armory or drill-room or rooms, for any regiment or other organization of the national guard of the state of New York, it shall be lawful for the comptroller of the city of New York to, and he shall, and the mayor, aldermen, and commonalty of the city of New York are hereby made liable to pay for such use and occupation, during such period as has not been paid for, such compensation as shall be determined to be fair and reasonable by a commission consisting of the mayor and comptroller of the city of New York and such commissioner of the department of taxes and assessments of the said city as the said comptroller shall, and he is hereby required to, designate, within ten days after the passage of this act; the determination of a majority to be the decision of the commission.

Claimants to be heard upon ten days' notice.

§ 2. Claimants may be heard before the commission upon ten days' notice to the department of finance, and upon the hearing, witnesses may be examined for and against the claim. The commissioners are, and each of them is, hereby authorized to administer an oath to witnesses. The attendance of witnesses may be compelled by subpœna, signed by any commissioner.

Determination of the commissioners to be filed.

§ 3. The commissioners, or a majority of them, shall certify and report in writing, and file in the office of the comptroller of the city of New York, their determination upon each claim brought before them, and such determination shall be final and binding upon all parties concerned.

The comptroller to issue bonds.

§ 4. The comptroller of the city of New York is hereby directed to borrow upon bonds of the mayor, aldermen, and commonalty of the city of New York, bearing interest at a rate not exceeding seven per cent. per annum, and payable at a period not to exceed three years from the date thereof, such amounts as shall be necessary to make all the payments herein provided for.

§ 5. This act shall take effect immediately.

Chapter 432.

AN ACT to provide for a further supply of pure and wholesome water for the twenty-third and twenty-fourth wards of the city of New York.

Passed May 27, 1876 ; three-fifths being present.

The People of the State of New York, represented in Senate and Assembly, do enact as follows :

Section 1. The commissioner of public works of the city of New York is hereby authorized to expend for materials and labor, and other services, in such manner as the said commissioner shall deem for the best interests of said city in laying pipes and doing such other things as may be necessary to the distribution of Croton water for the extinguishment of fires and all other purposes that may be required in the twenty-third and twenty-fourth wards of said city of New York, a sum not exceeding three hundred thousand dollars. The work connected with the laying of such pipe shall be done and performed by contract, entered into by the department of public works of said city, founded on sealed bids or proposals, made in compliance with public notice, duly advertised in the City Record ; said notice to be published at least ten days, and all such contracts when given shall be given to the lowest bidder, the terms of whose contract shall be settled by the counsel to the corporation as an act of preliminary specification to the bid or proposal, and who shall give security for the faithful performance of his contract in such amount as may be required, and the adequacy and sufficiency of said security shall, in addition to the justification and acknowledgment, be passed upon and determined by the comptroller of said city within twenty days from and after the declaration of the award of said contract. All bids or proposals shall be publicly opened by the officers advertising for the same, and in the presence of said comptroller :

Pipes, etc., for the distribution of Croton water in the 23d and 24th wards.

Work to be done by contract.

Bids when opened.

but the opening of the bids shall not be postponed if the comptroller shall, after due notice, fail to attend. If the

Acceptance of contract.

lowest bidder shall neglect or refuse to accept the contract within forty-eight hours after written notice that the same has been awarded to his bid or proposal, or if he accepts, but does not execute the contract, and give the proper security, it shall be readvertised and relet as above pro-

Work abandoned by contractor.

vided. In case any work shall be abandoned by the contractor, it shall be readvertised and relet by the commissioner of public works in the manner in this section

Bid to be rejected.

provided. And any bid shall be rejected which, if at the time it is submitted, is not accompanied by a certified check payable to the order of the comptroller of the city of New York, for an amount equal to one per cent. of the entire amount named in the bid, which said check shall be forfeited to the city in case the bid shall be accepted, and the bidder or bidders shall not furnish good and sufficient

Sureties.

sureties for the performance of the contract thereunder, and the said sureties shall not justify according to law; and upon the justification of the said sureties, the said check shall be returned to the contractor; and in either of such cases, it shall be lawful to readvertise for the performance of such work, and furnishing such supplies and materials, and to receive new bids or proposals therefor. The amount herein authorized to be expended is hereby declared to be in reduction to that extent of the amount authorized to be expended under chapter four hundred and seventy-seven of the laws of eighteen hundred and seventy-five.

Bonds to be issued.

§ 2. It shall be the duty of the comptroller of the city of New York, and he is hereby authorized and directed, to borrow upon bonds or stocks of the mayor, aldermen, and commonalty of the city of New York, such amounts as the commissioner of public works shall, from time to time, deem necessary to carry out the provisions of the first section of this act, not, however, exceeding in the whole the sum of three hundred thousand dollars. And the mayor and comptroller of said city of New York are hereby authorized and directed to sign such bonds; such bonds shall be entitled "Croton water main stock of the city of New York," and shall bear interest at a rate not exceeding seven per cent. per annum, and shall be redeemable in not less than ten nor more than fifty years from the date of their issue, as the said comptroller shall determine to be for the best interest of said city. Such bonds shall not be disposed of for less than the par value thereof, and it shall be the duty of the clerk of the common council of said city to countersign the same, and affix the seal of the city thereto. And the proper authorities of the city and county of New York are hereby authorized and directed to cause to be raised, from time to time, by tax upon the estates, real and personal, subject to taxation, in the city and county of New York, the sum of money which may be required to pay the interest on said bonds and to redeem them at maturity.

Bonds, how signed.

When redeemed.

§ 3. The money to be raised by virtue of this act, shall be applied and expended for the purposes authorized by this act, and for no other purpose whatever.

§ 4. The faith of the city and county of New York, and the revenues thereof, are hereby pledged for the payment of the interest of said bonds or stock, and the redemption of the principal of said debt hereby created, and the bonds authorized to be issued under this act.

Payment of interest of bonds.

§ 5. This act shall take effect immediately.

Chapter 433.

AN ACT to amend chapter fifty-six of the laws of eighteen hundred and seventy-one, entitled "An act to provide a further supply of pure and wholesome water for the city of New York."

Passed May 27, 1876; three-fifths being present.

The People of the State of New York, represented in Senate and Assembly, do enact as follows:

SECTION 1. Section eight of chapter fifty-six of the laws of eighteen hundred and seventy-one, entitled "An act to provide a further supply of pure and wholesome water for the city of New York, is hereby amended so as to read as follows:

§ 8. If, in executing any of the provisions of this act, it becomes necessary or proper to use, occupy, or overflow the ground now occupied by a public highway, the aforesaid mayor, aldermen, and commonalty may either raise the surface of such highway above the surface of the water, Title of land to be acquired. or acquire the title for and cause a new and convenient highway to be laid out and constructed in lieu thereof, provided said highway shall be located, subject to the approval of the board of supervisors of Putnam county, and the said commissioners shall make due and reasonable Allowance made. allowance to parties injuriously affected by the alteration on any road; said new highway shall be of as great width and as well drained and graded as the one discontinued. When such new highway has been completed, the said commissioner of public works shall deposit a map of the same in the office of the clerk of the town or of the towns in which said highway is located. The said new highway shall thereupon become a public highway in lieu of that occupied by the works constructed pursuant to this act.

§ 2. This act shall take effect immediately.

Chapter 434.

AN ACT to provide for the audit and payment of claims for repairs, printing, labor, and other incidental matters in and about public school buildings, incurred during the years eighteen hundred and sixty-nine, eighteen hundred and seventy, eighteen hundred and seventy-one, and eighteen hundred and seventy-two, by the trustees of the common schools of the several wards in the city of New York, and to provide means therefor.

Passed June 1, 1876 ; three-fifths being present.

The People of the State of New York, represented in Senate and Assembly, do enact as follows :

SECTION 1. The board of education of the city of New York are hereby authorized and required, within thirty days after the passage of this act, to audit and adjust the several claims which have heretofore been filed with the clerk of said board in the office of said board, for mechanics, services and other expenses relating to the school buildings under the charge of said board, and which remain unadjusted for the years eighteen hundred and sixty-nine, eighteen hundred and seventy, eighteen hundred and seventy-one, and eighteen hundred and seventy-two, which claims, in the aggregate, shall not exceed twenty-five thousand dollars. *Clerk of the board of education to audit claims unadjusted.*

§ 2. Within ninety days after the passage of this act the comptroller of the city of New York is hereby directed to borrow, on the credit of the mayor, aldermen, and commonalty of the city of New York, on bonds of the said city, to be denominated revenue bonds, and in anticipation of the collection of the taxes to be levied and imposed on the property, real and personal, subject to taxation in the city and county of New York for the year one thousand eight hundred and seventy-six, the sum of twenty-five thousand dollars, or so much thereof as may be necessary *Payment of, how made.*

for the purpose of paying the claims which are referred to in section one, and which shall be audited and adjusted by said board. The revenue bonds herein mentioned shall bear interest at the rate of not exceeding seven per cent. per annum.

§ 3. It shall be the duty of the said comptroller of the city of New York, from the moneys derived from the sale of said bonds, to pay the amount of such claims as he shall deem to be just, after the same have been allowed and certified to him as correct and just by the auditor of accounts in the finance department, and no claims referred to in section one shall be paid until after certification thereof is made to the finance department by the board of education.

To be certified to.

§ 4. The board of estimate and apportionment of the city of New York are hereby authorized, directed, and required to cause to be included in the taxes to be levied and raised in the said city of New York, for the year one thousand eight hundred and seventy-six, upon the estate subject to taxation in the city and county of New York, an amount sufficient to pay the revenue bonds herein directed to be issued by the said comptroller in anticipation of the collection of the said taxes, with all interest due or to become due thereon.

Payment of the bonds.

§ 5. For the purpose of this act, all acts or parts of acts inconsistent with this act are hereby repealed.

§ 6. This act shall take effect immediately.

Chapter 436.

AN ACT to amend chapter six hundred and four of the laws of eighteen hundred and seventy-four, entitled " An act to provide for the surveying, laying out, and monumenting of certain portions of the city and county of New York, and to provide means therefor.'

Passed June 2, 1876 ; three-fifths being present.

The People of the State of New York, represented in Senate and Assembly, do enact as follows :

SECTION 1. The second section of an act entitled " An act to provide for the surveying, laying out, and monu. menting of certain portions of the city and county of New York, and to provide means therefor," passed June fifth, eighteen hundred and seventy-four, is hereby amended by adding at the end thereof, the following : On the maps *Maps, how made.* or plans prepared and filed in accordance with the provisions of this act, the said commissioners of the department of public parks shall designate each street, avenue or road, as belonging to one of three classes. A street, avenue, or road of the first class shall be such as in the judgment of said commissioners, is or may be needed for the convenience of the general public, either as a main route of travel, or for drainage. The streets of this class may be opened by the board or the department of the city government having control of such opening, whenever in their opinion the interest of the public demands such opening or grading. A street, avenue, or road of the second class shall be such *Street or avenue, how opened.* as in the judgment of said commissioners is or may be needed for the use or convenience of the inhabitants of certain areas or districts, as thoroughfares but which are not main routes of travel. Streets of this class shall be opened only on the petition of the owners of at least one third of the linear feet of frontage on such streets, and the streets intersecting the same for five hundred feet in each direction from such intersection. A street, avenue, or road of the third class shall be such as in the judgment of the said commissioners is or may be needed only for the subdivision of the property through which it passes. Streets of this class shall be opened or graded only on the petition of the owners of at least three-fourths of the linear feet of frontage on such streets.

§ 2. This act shall take effect immediately.

Chapter 447.

AN ACT in relation to Riverside avenue and park in the city of New York.

Passed June 2, 1876; three-fifths being present.

The People of the State of New York, represented in Senate and Assembly, do enact as follows:

Payment for labor and material. SECTION 1. The comptroller of the city of New York is hereby authorized and directed to pay for any work, services, or material furnished, or to be furnished under any contract or contracts for improving the avenue known as Riverside avenue, in the city of New York, as laid out under the second section of chapter eight hundred and fifty of the laws of eighteen hundred and seventy-three, and shown upon a map thereof, filed under the provisions of said section, on the twenty-third day of February, in the year one thousand eight hundred and seventy-five, by the construction of the roadways, curb and gutter and sidewalks, which have been or may be adopted by the department of parks; and in order to enable the said comptroller to make such payments, he is hereby authorized, empowered, and directed to borrow from time to time, in the name of the mayor, aldermen, and commonalty of

the city of New York, by the issue of bonds bearing Bonds to be issued.
such rate of interest as he may deem proper, not exceeding
seven per cent. per annum, such sums as shall be necessary
to pay all expenses incurred or to be incurred, as aforesaid ;
the expenses of such work shall be assessed by the board Assessments made.
of assessors, of said city, on the property benefited, and
the money collected by such assessment is hereby pledged
for the redemption of the bonds so to be issued.

§ 2. The whole of the land embraced within the bound- Declared one of the parks of the city of New York.
aries of Riverside avenue, is hereby declared to be one of
the parks and public places in the city of New York, and
shall be under the control and management of the department of parks of said city, subject to the provisions of the
first section of this act in respect to the roadways, curb
and gutter, and sidewalks therein mentioned.

§ 3. This act shall take effect immediately.